TREATISE OF METAPHYSICAL MARTIAL ARTS

The Art that began in the Heavens

BY M.J. WALKER

Wisdom is the stability of all, for knowledge is the whole law.

1

SPECIAL THANKS & GRATITUDE

One love to all who I have gained wisdom from throughout my life and journey. In this world of tests, I will not give up without a fight. Peace in darkness and as always... #SKOD

Sacred Knowledge Over Delusion

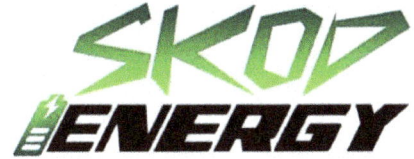

DEDICATION

This book is dedicated to my lovely wife. Years of hard work, money, and energy spent have allowed me to accomplish much, but without the anchor in my life, I would not be where I am today. Truly, If I can inspire one soul from this writing... I have done enough.

TABLE OF CONTENTS

Chapter 1: Love of Wisdom

Chapter 2: The Art of War or The Skillful Master

Chapter 3: The Lesser Knowledge

Chapter 4: Mind, Creation, Self-Expression

Chapter 5: The Electric Idea

Chapter 6: The Temple, The Soul, The Spirit

Chapter 7: The Inborn Powers of Man

Chapter 8: The Battle of the Gods

❖ REFERENCES

KING JAMES BIBLE OT

1. The Book of Ecclesiastes
2. The Book of Genesis
3. The Book of Deuteronomy
4. The Book of Psalms
5. The Book of Isaiah

KING JAMES BIBLE NT

1. The Gospel of Matthew
2. The Gospel of John
3. The Book of Acts
4. The Book of Hebrews
5. The Book of Philippians
6. The Book of Corinthians
7. The Book of Galatians
8. The Book of Revelation

THE NAG HAMMADI SCRIPTURES

1. Coptic Gospel of Thomas
2. Acts of Peter
3. Gospel of Judas
4. Acts of The Apostles
5. Gospel of Phillip

ANCIENT TABLETS & PAPYRUS

1. The Emerald Tablets of Thoth the Atlantean
2. The Lost Book of Enki
3. The Epic of Gilgamesh
4. The Battle of Gods and Men
5. The Dead Sea Scrolls

APOCRYPHAL BOOKS

1. The Book of Adam and Eve
2. The Book of Jubilees
3. The Book of Jasher
4. The Testament of the Twelve Patriarchs

PSEUDEPIGRAPHA BOOKS

1. The 1st Book of Enoch
2. The 2nd Book of Enoch

PHILOSOPHICAL & HISTORICAL BOOKS

1. The Tao of Jeet Kune do
2. Jesus and the Essenes
3. Tree of Knowledge
4. The Aquarian Gospel of Jesus the Christ
5. The Kyballion
6. The Secret Teachings of All Ages
7. As A Man Thinketh
8. The Healing Power of Hand Mudras
9. Oxford English Dictionary
10. Zondervan Bible dictionary
11. Encyclopedia Britannica

FAMOUS QUOTES

1. French Historian Auguste Vallet de Viriville

2. American Author Phyllis Mcginley
3. American Poet Robert Frost
4. Polymath Leonardo Da Vinci
5. Scientist Neil DeGrasse

ARTICLE STUDY LINKS

1. *Gems in style Blog* https://gemsinstyle.com/blogs/news/sun-moon-gold-silver-celestial-dialectic-and-the-art-of-balance

2. *Psychologist*   *Allen*   *Cohen* https://www.cia.gov/readingroom/document/nsa-rdp96x00790r000100040008-6

3. *Copenhagen*   *Interpretation*   *article* https://www.lode.de/blog/copenhagen-interpretation

4. *Daryl*   *Ben*   *Cornell*   *Chronicle* https://news.cornell.edu/stories/2010/12/study-looks-brains-ability-see-future

5. *Eleanor*   *Criswell*   *psychic*   *liberation* https://www.cia.gov/readingroom/document/nsa-rdp96x00790r000100040008-6

6. *Air*   *Force*   *High*   *Energy*   *Laser*   *2019*   *Article* https://www.rtx.com/raytheon/what-we-do/integrated-air-and-missile-defense/lasers

❖ PREFACE

There have been countless volumes of introductory literature concerning ancient philosophies and spiritual practices alluding to the supernatural phenomena within humankind. A phenomenon, though spiritual and cosmic, having its roots in the infinite mind within the primordial, is also physical, showing the dimensions of its power through man's bodily tools and extremities. If only Mankind knew how to use his appendages, it would open a world that is likened to Pandora's box. This is neither instructions nor a list of rules for the obtainment of such forces; rather, it is a collection of philosophic ideals gained from the study of many ancient texts and customs compiled together to shed light on one of the most interesting and ancient topics of all time. This work is not complete; however, in its incompleteness, we begin to piece together the art of thought, creation, and life. The present work attempts to supply the reader with the tools necessary to reach into the debts of the knowledge within, far greater than previously understood.

This treatise was compiled from years of study, beginning in the early year of 2019, and continuing throughout this present time. The reason this endeavor needed to be cultivated for such a long time is that I needed to find the right concepts and thought forms to bring about an ideal that is solely attributed to my purpose and perspective. Not according to what a religious leader or superior says or some other outside entity, but according to what my soul expresses as "the truth." Meditation and deep thought were the seeds planted in mental earth for such a creation. Throughout much of my early years of life, my knowledge of the spiritual realm and martial arts has been widely influenced by outside sources. There is only so much one can do in his youth to obtain that which his soul needs. Even as a young boy, I have had glimpses of the cosmic supernatural via memory and experience, but as I matured in age, I found that the greatest essence of knowledge is found within, expressed through a deep oneness of self-acclimation. However, with the aid of the arcana writings of ancient religious sects, mystery schools of thought, and Apocryphal literature belonging to the early Hebrews, Brahmins, Greeks, Romans, and Egyptians, the entire puzzle began to reveal itself. No longer would the occult truths of the glorious hierophants of old elude us, and no longer would the relics of a bygone society be stripped from our wanting eyes. Together, they cultivated a masterpiece of what some have called fantasy and fiction, while others have considered it a veracious corporeality. However you decide to label the notion, it cannot be refuted that Hollywood has cast a shadow of mystery, illusion, and fantasy with their part in the dissemination of legends.

As the mystics of old, the great storytellers of humanity have said, and I passionately believe this. "Behind every myth lies a truth; beyond every legend is a reality, as radiant and sometimes as chilling as the story itself." (see the writings of

Phyllis McGinley) I have said above previously that many avenues of information have been assessed for the completion of this work, and while these texts and my opinions are confirmed by various authors, philosophers, theologians, and enlightened sages, I found that truth is one but God. Verily, truth is in the eye of the beholder, for perspective with partiality renders misrepresentation. The great Philosopher and initiate Bruce Lee, Famously Called the Dragon, not only for his fierceness in Art but also for his illuminated wisdom and knowledge, which transcended race, skin, and creed. He stated once in his short but magnificent life, "Truth has no path. Truth is living and, therefore, changing. It has no resting place, no form, no organized institution, no philosophy. When you see that, you will understand that this living thing is also what you are. You cannot express and be alive through static, put together forms, or through stylized movement." (See the Tao of Jeet Kune Do) If man could re-discover what was lost from the days of old and somehow find a way to "BE," what then would stop him from creating the world he so desires? What then, would stop him from unlocking the fairytale that is Life? As Solomon, the wise Israelite magician, hermeticist, alchemist, and priest-king in his ecclesiastical writing said, "and further by these my son be admonished of the making of many books there is no end, and much study is weariness of the flesh." (see the book of Ecclesiastes) The great Magician did not say this to dissuade souls from the everlasting quest for knowledge but rather to spark a continuous fire that incessantly burns flames fed with the bread of life.

I was raised in an average single-family home with a working father who struggled with his own insecurities and imperfections, but one day somehow, he practically rose from the dead in the streets of Camden, New Jersey. Like a miracle introduced us to the Baptist Christian church, and becoming a Reverend set the tone for me to pursue a religious yet philosophic life. Although I did not realize it, my journey would begin from this foundation. At one point in my life, my father was a huge fan of the old martial arts movies from the 70s and 80s, Bruce Lee being the main attraction. I could also remember Shownuff and his Wiley antics. Watching his pursuit of Bruce Lee Roy was a family favorite in my household. My father was a self-proclaimed martial artist with many tales of neighborhood brawls and legendary conditioning sessions with nature that would leave my imagination thriving for more. He would, at times, play around with all the kids on our hometown block, egging them on to attack him. When they would answer his call and surround him, me included, I would think the odds favor the mighty in numbers. On the contrary, only one number mattered! As soon as we started the pressure, you would see the spinning heel kicks and the blazing fast reflexes of a home-born warrior. You see, fighters are born; their destiny is written in the stars and spoken within the halls of the great warrior souls of all time. Little did I know just how far into the artistry I would go. Alongside my father was my mother. Strong and willed, yet when my father was absent due to incarceration, she single-handedly kept myself and my two other siblings (me being the youngest child at that time) safe, fed, and taken care of. Through hard work and sheer determination, I watched my mother keep a full-time job, all while attending nursing school and eventually earning her Nursing Degree. I learned persistence, patience, and resilience from this woman. Not only are these excellent qualities of a man but also excellent qualities of a philosophic martial artist. The mind is meant to be in all, for it is your ment-all or in other words your mental.

DISCLAIMER

I do not make any claim for either the infallibility or originality of any statement herein contained; rather, I record my thoughts, opinions, and studies with all purity of heart, praying that the magnitude of wisdom would be endowed on the reader. The possibilities of those who gain knowledge from a work such as this are all the fuel needed for the dissemination of my ideas and concepts. Having no demographic of my own, I have learned to study all information to leave no stone unturned. If I assuredly keep my research, investigation, and purity of heart, then I shall be able to discern between duality, good and evil, left and right, or up and down.

INTRODUCTION TO THE MYSTERY ART||

Wisdom is the stability of all. Illumination is the measure of stability and consistency, for knowledge is the whole law.

The concepts of life and nature and the pervading force have long been a part of the mysteries of art. In fact, I have come to find that most of the questions humankind has sought are answered by the magnificent environment around us. Nature and the correspondence of man is one of the biggest mysteries plaguing the thoughts of the curious. What is spirituality? What are the origins of martial arts, and do these two components complement each other in any way, or are they one? Somehow, we have lost discernment of the hidden glory nature teaches us through its symbolic cyclic complexion. In consideration of this obvious blunder, we adhere to an excellent quote from the dragon Bruce Lee. "To Understand, you must study all-natural movements of living things." (see the Tao of Jeet Kune Do) In this regard, the Art that we speak of holds both beauty and wisdom but not without expression, and what is expression but the fundamental ethos of everything that exists. Beauty is eloquently illustrated under the terms of harmony, manifesting its own intrinsic nature in the world of form. (See the Pythagorean theory of music and color) Jesus, whom I will reference numerous times in this work, was a man of many magical accomplishments; often, he expands on the origin of all things, but in one of the most groundbreaking controversial texts shrouded from the eyes of man, It is said from the Essene initiate, "If anyone asks you where you come from, that is (being our origin and basis of creation) we are to respond to them we come from light." (See the Coptic Gospel of Thomas) For that light was the creative life of men. Comprised in that light was the origin of arithmetic and occult mathematics, sacred geometry, Quantum Science, and Cosmic thought, along with all the vital sources of energy that embody the building blocks of the universe.

You ask how I can make such an assertion. Well, these secret natural sciences were proven as fact as far back as the ancient Assyrians, who were making astonishing cosmic observations, and the Egyptians, who were said to possess the elixirs of life and sorcerer's stone. Lastly, the Dogon Tribe, who were said to have the origin of humans being seeded on this planet, and extraterrestrial encounters and voyages! Therefore, Prior to diving directly into the Philosophical and Metaphysical origins of martial arts, it is fair that a disclaimer is made. This book will be a collection of findings throughout my studies on the subject at hand. I will add excerpts from various writings from other well-known philosophers, mystics, theologians, historians, etc., as I have done in the above paragraphs. My intention is not to indoctrinate the reader into a school of thought, yet I will reveal hidden truths within these words, which have been heard by many, but only a few have been privileged to discern. The subject at hand has been a lifelong journey of mine supported throughout my early years of fantasy, imagination, and anime. It seems martial arts and the supernatural power behind it have truly revolutionized the minds of the curious and unexplained. There will be many points of view that you may have never entertained before. You will hear terms and words that may be against your programming, causing a glitch in the reader's psyche. Embrace the unknown, for in that space, your creativity will permeate. Your mind and soul will begin to receive the answers that it has been waiting for since your incarnation into this physical plane. If you believe in that perspective.

Throughout this text, you will hear the terms Kungfu and Martial arts. For now, I will discuss both terms as individual concepts, but as the writing goes on, these terms will be mentioned in one thought form. To the wise, these thought forms are everything, for they originated in the same Divinity of space as the ever-expanding mind which ignited the first thought! Respectively, Ancient spirituality, Kungfu, and Martial Arts are likened to poetic manuscripts teaching the soul the internal cheat codes of energy manipulation, ascension, Spirituality, health, love, chaos, order, and justice. Trigger warning: the words Occult and Esoteric will be used in the writing. I am sure you have heard of it already. Those who suffer from cognitive dissonance will automatically heave up defenses to impede what is being presented. Do not be this guy; our handlers and programmers are familiar with our propensity for liberation through faith and trust. So, they instill boundaries inside the psyche of men and women. These boundaries are from authority figures, who know that if activated, their own mind will fight against them before transitioning into a new and more balanced school of thought. In other words, what we are about to discuss, to the un-learned, is nothing short of verbal wickedness, but to the informed and the enlightened, it is secret and privileged. Phrases like Dark sayings or Allegories will be used in this text. We will cover the three lower divisions in humankind and the way they correspond with the thought of Kungfu and Martial Arts.

The Spirit, The Soul, and The Body are sometimes called the trinity in man. The premise of this is to expand the way we think concerning the subject of Cosmic Fighting and how its origins in the heavens can enlighten us on the way we use it today. I would like to introduce a metaphysical, anatomical, and physiological outlook concerning the use of one's mind and its mix with Divine thought. As everything originates in thought, the great dragon from the West, Bruce Lee, exclaimed in his Tao of Jeet Kune do, "Would we could strike with our eyes" and then went on to say, "sharpen the psychic power of seeing in order to act at once in accordance with what you see. Seeing takes place within the inner mind." Thus, we can begin to understand Mind over matter. I believe as first the spiritual, then the Material, so should the understanding of the art. As the great Paul, the man who was blind and then could see, said in his letter to the church of Corinth, "However the spiritual (pertaining to the immortal life) is not first but the physical (which is the mortal life) then the spiritual." To the literal reader, this would seem quite disagreeable, but on the contrary, the wise fathom the illusional allegory. We know spirit and soul are the harbinger of the body, but the body is needed to experience the five senses. Paul is not speaking in terms of creation but rather in the cosmic cycle of the involution of soul to body and evolution of body to spirit. (see the epistle to the Corinthians)

Manly P. Hall states in his writing, "Both god and man have a twofold constitution, of which the superior part is invisible and the inferior visible." (see the secret teachings of all ages). Thus, I believe Martial Arts, Kungfu, and true sacred religion are different but one and the same, and the "energy" of life," known as the light, from the beginning is the source of all things in creation. Contained within it was this electric "idea." I will elaborate, I Am not bound by any one way of thinking; rather, I accept all and do not reject knowledge. A great American poet and writer once said, "Education is the ability to listen to almost anything without losing your temper or your self-confidence." (see the works of Robert Frost) If it proves to be profitable, then I have gained divine wisdom. I adopt what is useful and inner stand on what does not fit my expression. It can be Secular, Scientific, biblical, poetic, philosophical, or metaphysical. As long as it is edifying and completes my thought, which is light, then we shall be fruitful. There is something special about setting your mentality in such a way that the biggest waves cannot disrupt your peace. Come with me as we embark on a journey of little speculation, which leads to deeper conquests. Articulation, that being words which are spells, cymatics incantations of eloquence. Lastly, revelation and mystery unfold in the reality of life. The philosophers say that when there is no center and no circumference, there is truth. When you freely express yourself, you are the total style. (See Tao of Jeet Kune DO) The matrix and its agents who instill your beliefs are bound by cosmic law, and only through these laws can we use the power within. I AM the Neo of my story and timeline, and so are you...

LET US CREATE.

CH. 1
THE LOVE OF WISDOM | |

THE ENVIRONMENT CREATES THE EXPERIENCE, AND THE EXPERIENCE MAKES LIFE MEANINGFUL

A man who desires wisdom will desire philosophy, for philosophy is the olive branch of knowledge extended to those bold enough to reach. This statement is about one of the most famous occult paintings, which was brilliantly illustrated by Michelangelo in his creation of Adam in the Sistine Chapel. Hidden in this artwork is yet the single and most important gem symbolically comprehended for the soul that wished to be initiated into the mysteries of wisdom, knowledge, and light. This knowledge corresponds with the philosophers' stone or the holy grail in alchemical resolution. Quoted from the intellectual literature of old, "The philosopher stone is really the philosophical stone, for philosophy is truly likened to a magical jewel its touch transmutes base substances into priceless gems like itself." (See the writings of Manly P Hall). Philosophy, when broken down to its core, refers to a school of thought pertaining to a particular subject or experience. When we look at its etymology, the root word in the Greek is "philos," meaning love, and "Sophia" meaning wisdom. (See Oxford English Dictionary) According to biblical and gnostic definitions, wisdom refers to the Holy Spirit, which is the Divine feminine aspect of the trinary emanation of the universal god. Ideally, martial arts can be broken down into three divisions of philosophy (Similar to the three divisions of man, which we will cover later). This school of thought is compounded with soul truths that, when realized, man can be lifted to a higher state of being, therefore elevating awareness.

The first is the chief commander's self-I AM realization. This corresponds with the root chakra in Hindu and yogi traditions. The individual wishing to undergo the philosophic life of martial arts must be aware of who and what he is, both externally and internally. The battle is first within the mind and subsequently the body and all other material surroundings, for your thoughts govern and create the human experience. As James Allen gracefully stated in his self-help writing of thought, "The outer world of circumstance shapes itself to the inner world of thought, and both pleasant and unpleasant external conditions are factors which make for the ultimate good of the individual." (See As a Man Thinketh) The master is one who controls the mind in thought, word, and deed. Temperance and patience are the most marvelous of virtues; however, they are not required to seek but rather to be initiated into the highest order of self-realization. It is something that everyone must learn. The individual man or woman who earns self-control is indeed a master artist. Painting the picture of his or her desires at will. Art is an expression of life and transcends both time and space. "We must employ our own souls through art to give a new meaning to nature or the world." (See Tao of Jeet Kune do the art of soul). A patient martial artist is likened to a wise serpent gazing upon the eyes of his enemy. Balanced with calmness from the force within and mastery of thought, the strike of the serpent is as lightning, and his defense is as the wind. A martial artist must relinquish all egotistical emotional trauma attached to his soul through mental hijacking or energetic karma of past experiences. I speak unto you, a parable. Confidence in self! Speak slowly to hear the hidden spell within. Confide in self! Build yourself, create yourself, love yourself, take care of yourself, and be honest with yourself. Only then can the world around you be changed. A philosophic martial artist is not swayed by what he sees; he is only swayed by what he understands, and only then does he realize his purpose. Here sits the golden scepter of rulership inside the mind of a god. When your eye is single, your entire body will be full of light. A wonderful allegory for the building of self-adulation and transmutation. (See the gospels of the New Testament)

The Second is authenticity in truth. Authenticity is the outward personification of Honesty. Being honest with oneself about internal shortcomings, doubts, fears, and trauma is likened to the admonition of one's sins and is the first alongside self-realization. Fear is the weed that chokes the plant of life from growth. It is said, written by the Wise James Allen, "Thoughts of doubt and fear never accomplished anything, and never can. They always lead to failure. Purpose, energy, power to do, and all strong thought cease when doubt and fear creep in." He goes on to state, "The will to do springs from the knowledge that we can do. Doubt and fear are the greatest enemies of knowledge, and he who encourages them, who does not slay them, thwarts himself in every step." Lastly, he affirms,

"He who has conquered doubt and fear has conquered failure. His every thought is allied with power, and all difficulties are bravely met and wisely overcome." (See As a Man Thinketh) When one carries himself as an original authentic being, one's own particular gifts will be realized and disseminated. Gifts that were smothered due to intrusive beliefs placed upon men will begin to awaken those who slumber. Naturally, in the body, with its original authentic design, lies the magic of the ever-expanding mind.

Have you seen the movie Lucy? What about Limitless? How about the early 2000 animated show Jimmy neutron and his iconic brain blast? I know you have heard of that! Emblematic of a god-like transformation, billions of genetic materials have the capability to combust and explode, bringing with them the knowledge and light your soul came to earth to share. Moreover, the sages have always known the capabilities of man and his birth-rite saying, "Man is a thought of God; all thoughts of God are infinite. They are not measured up by time for things that are concerned with time begin and end." (See the Aquarian gospel of Jesus the Christ) As an authentic man, in front of his fellow peers, you will find the testament of character and will. This man has identified with himself beyond the stigma and labels and yet feels comfortable identifying with nothing, therefore being all things. To become all things, this is a level of enlightenment a man can reach when his own egotistical self-centeredness does not stop him from empathy, love, harmony, and kindness. Bruce Lee, the dragon, once said this harmonic statement, "A fateful process is set in motion when the individual is released to the freedom of his own impotence and left to justify his existence by his own efforts. The individual, on his own, striving to realize himself and prove his worth, has created all that is great in literature, art, music, science, and technology. This autonomous individual also, when he can neither realize himself nor justify his existence by his own efforts, is a breeding ground of frustration and the seed of the convulsion that shakes our world to its foundation." (See Tao of Jeet Kune DO)

Truly, nature is free, and the fruits of her womb should be disseminated amongst all people regardless of religious, economic, financial, and cultural differences embedded in the psyche of each soul incarnating in this realm. The dragon also has a very great statement I would like to add regarding the attack on the psyche of man. "One can never be the master of his technical knowledge unless all his psychic hindrances are removed, and he can keep his mind in a state of emptiness or fluidity, even purged of whatever technique he has obtained." (See Tao of Jeet Kune Do) This is the ultimate goal of oneness. Referenced in the epistle text of the Bible, spoken by Paul, the man who was made blind by Christ, who is the light, and yet in darkness could see the shining brightness of the morning star and thus drink of his enlightened wisdom. "To the weak became I as weak, that I might win the weak, I have become all things to All people, so that I may by all means gain some." (see the epistle to the church of Corinth). Again, he stated a similar allegory concerning the eternal identity of the soul and salvation, "there is neither Jew nor Greek, Bond or free, male nor female, for ye are all one in Christ Jesus" (See the epistle to the church of Galatia). The soul transcends the body, mind over matter, and spirit over mind. We can also find the same reference to oneness or becoming all things in Buddhist culture. Here summarized are the eight-fold path requirements to eliminate suffering by correcting false values and giving true knowledge of life. Number 1: You must have the right views and understanding. Number 2: You must have the right purpose or aspiration. Number 3: You must build upon the right speech speak as to aim. Number 4: You must keep the right conduct and actions. Number 5: You must have the right vocation and livelihood, and it must not conflict with your healing. Number 6: You must make the right effort. Healing must be sustained. Number 7: you must have the right awareness. This is mind control. Number 8: you must have the right concentration to meditate deep in the mind. (See Tao of Jeet kune Do) All of these virtues allow you to be a creator in a world full of wasters. The nonchalant and the slothful will go about life with the propensity to accept whatever is given to them instead of manifesting what they will. I speak a parable unto you: the rain droplet, which was once whole, has now become the ocean, and the place from whence it came, and where it will go...contains its origin. This parable of water, the most essential element by which all life, terrestrial and extra-terrestrial, is sustained, corresponds with the soul and cyclic nature.

The final division is the infallible process of mental, spiritual regeneration, and physical transmutation. In this philosophy, A man who wishes to live the life of a martial artist will need to comprehend its philosophical origins, thereby properly expressing himself without corruption. All ancient knowledge is profitable, but accompanied by it is the equal perversion of that same energy. So, in theory, a man who is harmonious in thought will always need to be on guard from the double edge sword of duality. Corruption is instability within the mind and the inability to control the desires of the vessel. The hidden truths of martial arts are also soul truths that empower its users to divine capabilities. The body is yet the instrument of the mind, and the mind is engulfed within the soul during its journey in the celestial realms and after its journey within the mundane and arcane (the physical realm), as the 33-degree mason and philosopher Manly. P. Hall said in his closing remarks within the secret teachings of all ages. "The soul of man has not yet been deprived of its wings; They are merely folded under his garment of flesh. Philosophy is ever that magic power which, surrendering the vessel of clay, releases the soul from its bondage to habit and perversion." Realizing everything is relative, I gathered this hypothesis: these martial arts hidden truths, which, when vibrating in a proper harmonious frequency with them, will constitute the manipulation of the four elements, and interestingly enough, this corresponds with the complete regeneration of the human soul and body. The principles left on earth by these wise sages throughout the ages have perpetuated countless magical men and women who were called "magicians, sorcerers, witches, and warlocks for having the secret knowledge of the gods.

You may be wondering how we can link these spiritual texts to something as practical as martial arts. What I want you to realize is that this all has oneness in the mind. Even magical powers and manipulation of chi energy! Anything you can think of in any way you would like to utilize your external energy can be accomplished through the mastery of the mind (the brain) and emotions (the heart). The mighty men of old and great warriors of valor all understood the power of oneness and emotional control. Ten men could slay ten thousand. Ancient Demi gods battled with skill and might. As written in the Torah of the Hebrews, "How could one have chased a thousand and two have put ten thousand to flight unless their rock had sold them, and the lord had given them up." (see the writings of Deuteronomy) It seems the lord of the Hebrews had an actual hand in the battles indicated by the scripture above. "Had it not been for the Lord who was on my side" an orthodox Christian hymn seems to be a literal theme amongst the ancient text, or was the dna of the humans at that time more powerful than the people of today? Were the ancient Israelites Along with the other nations of the world literally mixed with the dna of the gods? All amazing theories and questions. The physical aspect is always a product of the spiritual. The book of Revelation and Daniel, one of the wisest allegorical texts ever recorded, speaks of spiritual beasts rising up out of the sea, commanding power and might amongst the world of men. It shows the spiritual origin of the material and how its higher frequency attributes physically manifest their will upon this plane of existence. In other words, A spiritual action will cause a physical reaction and manifestation. The natural law of cause and effect. As with creation, the invisible proceeded to the visible, likewise the soul truths before the physical mastery of body, weaponry, and hand combat. The latter is all a part of the coined term "lesser knowledge" revealed unto the world of men in the hidden literature of Enoch the Scribe.

Among these erroneous names mentioned above, rightly titled for some but wrongfully to others, are the likes of Simon Peter, the one who sliced off the ear of the centurion and violently caused the disposition of Simon Magus, the magician in the battle of the two powers. (See the Acts of Peter) Pythagoras, called the First Philosopher, healed his patients through music therapy and color manipulation; he was also likened to the savior of the Hebrew people symbolically, according to legend. (See the secret teachings of all ages) Thoth, the Atlantean master magician coined the god of wisdom, lived and ruled for over 16000 years, transferring his consciousness through different avatars, Astro projecting, conquering space-time through the corners of light. (See the Emerald Tablets of Thoth the Atlantean) Also written in the legends, Thoth, known as Ninggishzidda, battled adversaries and healed heroes with magic. "From his celestial boat, Ningishzidda came down to save the hero for his mother. With magic powers, Ningishzidda, the poison to benevolent blood, converted." Written and encoded in the legends, myths, and story-tales of old is the goldmine for the soul and catalyst for the cosmic serpent fire, also known as the baptism of fire or the rushing on slot of the Holy Spirit and her cloven tongues of fire written of in the gospels. (see the acts of the apostles)

Meditation is an Art that unlocks the essence buried within man. Slow the chaos of the mind and enter the tranquility of Silence. A wise mathematician once said, "Most of man's problems stem from his inability to sit in a quiet room alone. (See the works of Blaise Pascal). The life of a philosophic martial artist is a disciplined life cultured through travels and experiences; the knowledge gained from these different environments will make the experience meaningful on a soul level, mental level, and social level. Lifting the veil to a world full of possibilities where the rule of law is Heart. Metaphysically, the heart is Christ, divine love, king and savior, and the sun and morning star within each of us. Numerically, the number 4. This is the number of laws and order corresponding with the 4th chakra. Green, the precious emerald stone of the tribe of Judah, who, according to the ancient text, is the 4th son of Israel, formerly known as Jacob, and king of the twelve tribes. The name in itself is an Allegory for the god man, or Superhuman, in terms of heightened abilities and sensory observatories. According to many ancient Kemet hidden philosophies, Israel is a cipher containing the divine feminine aspect known as ISIS, the mother god, the divine Male Aspect known as RA, the father god, and the Spirit or Ether, known to all ancients as EL. When Jacob received a new name after wrestling the holy angel, a wonderful transformation occurred.

Symbolically and culturally, a name constitutes a duty or nature. Nature is defined not only as the pervading physical force that causes and regulates natural phenomena, but it also represents the innate or essential qualities or character of a person or animal. Nature, in the archaic sense, is a person of a specified character. Moreover, according to the Zondervan bible dictionary, a name was only given by a person in a position of authority and signified that the person named was appointed to a particular position, function, or relationship. This is no anomaly because we can find many ancient texts alluding to powerful gods or angels visiting religious patriarchs and hierophants and bestowing a new name upon the holy initiate. As it is written in the book of the Hebrews, the god of Abram changed his name to reflect his destiny! (see the book of genesis) This would mean that, with Jacob receiving a new name or nature, he received a higher constitution or a transformation to his innate original power, therefore confirming the holy text according to the outward and also the inward. These masters who accomplish this great task as Jacob did are often called the enlightened minds who can bend reality and create at will. They tend to be Master healers, master teachers, master builders, multi-talented, and very intellectual. A philosophic martial artist will be able to comprehend time in such a manner that from point A to point Z is a matter of perspective, on and off the field of battle. Prosperity and abundance can manifest in many ways according to their innate desire fully cultivated to be placed on display for the consciously aware mind. A lifetime is but a space, and in a space, we execute.

CH.2
THE ART OF WAR OR THE SKILLFUL MASTER | |

MEN AND WOMEN ARE BORN INTO THIS WORLD, CREATED WITH EVERYTHING ALREADY INSIDE. WE DO NOT NEED ANY OUTSIDE INFLUENCE TO ACHIEVE SPIRITUALITY. WE NEED ONLY TO STRENGTHEN THE CONNECTION TO SELF, SOUL, AND SPIRIT.

In this section, I will briefly attempt to elaborate on the differences between KungFu and Martial Arts. They are very distinct yet have similarities and are usually conjoined together as being one and the same. This may have been the case due to those who run modern society and entertainment, or maybe it was something only understood by a few and passed down through the ages and generations as such, with levels that require initiation for its secrets. The mystery of the topic is something we can only begin to uncover. Looking at the etymology of "KungFu or GongFu," we find that it is comprised of two words. "Gong" means achievement, Merit, Skill, or art, and "Fu" means time spent. This especially refers to self-defense; however, it is not limited to that. The Higher meaning beyond the surface states that Kung Fu can be any skill or talent acquired through serious training. It doesn't matter what profession a person has or what avenue one wants to express oneself in; true kung fu is any art. Like riding a bike in a marathon or mountain climbing, or even something as calm as breathing properly and listening intensively, is an art. Each has its own resonation and vibration but is classified under the same discipline, and that is "Art." The Late great Polymath of the High

Renaissance, who was also a world renown painter, draftsman, engineer, scientist, theorist, sculptor, and architect, stated a very famous saying which, when meditated on, would revolutionize the way the world thinks concerning art, "to develop a complete mind: study the science of art; study the art of science. Learn how to see. Realize that everything connects to everything." (See the works of Leonardo da Vinci)

In other words, the term Kung Fu signifies the proper preparation for any performance or any skillful endeavor without interference from the intellect or emotions. Making art an outward manifestation of a soulful inward progression (Please see the encyclopedia Brittanica Definition of KungFu) In my research, I find that KungFu can be classified under three main factions. In the chief sense, the faction of ancient philosophy, the way of life and love. Here, we find many allegories and hidden soul truths from all nations and peoples. We find secrets of religion and spirituality that could bring power when uttered to the worthy. In the more obvious sense, the faction of the material realm is the body and all its constitutions. Here, one learns the plainer knowledge; through toil and sacrifice, he reaches countless plateaus, but if he has not mastered the first or even tried to become aware of this faculty, he will lack in his full dimension of conduct. Lastly, the final sense is the faction of energetic manipulation. Here, after having mastered the afore-mentioned factions prior to the latter, we find that it is but a mixture of the first listed factions. The manifestation of all three is creation and balance. Through the entirety of this writing, we will uncover and disseminate many hidden meanings and truths. Some are allegorical, others spiritual, profane to some, and magical to others, but to the individual who will seek the meaning of such a thought, he must, in turn, seek himself. Kung fu and martial arts are within the mastermind. This is the level of spiritual awareness that has been spoken of throughout generations and all through the ages. Man could achieve this if he chooses.

The Master mind is one without the interference of Intellect or emotion. In biblical philosophy, the carnal Mind, or Logical Brain, is the interference. This holds the ego attached to the five senses with which we can experience this material projection. If the ego is unchecked, the carnal mind delivers shackles and fetters to the mind of one aspiring for elevation. He who is entrusted with the mind of the master is one that is not subject to the ways of the lower self or one that is not subject to any involuntary emotions, whether justified or unjustified. This would mean, theoretically, the outside influences of nature, economic, political, and religious constructs are but a breeze in the wind to the master mind. Now, when we deep dive into the term Martial Arts and get to its origins and etymology, The Word "Martial" has its roots in Latin, "Martialis" meaning War-like or pertaining to war. The Roman God of War is associated with the planet Mars. This is interesting in itself, seeing as the idea of martial arts in the heavens, I will broadcast throughout this text. Mars also corresponds to the Anunnaki God Nergal, son of Enlil Lord of the Edin, also known as Yahweh or IAM That I AM by the Hebrews. Nergal is mentioned in the bible as a deity of the city of Cuth. In the Mesopotamian religion, Irra the god of scorched earth and war. Ancient allegories and legends inscribed on stone tablets made of gold or in the ancient mysteries spoken only in secret but written on papyri for the initiated held the ancient doctrine of life, the secrets of man hidden. The origins of everything, the powers within, and the powers without. The great mystic Manly P. Hall stated in his (The secret teachings of all ages) that each planetary energy in creation effects the created on the physical plane, manipulating their bodies with cosmic energy, which in tune would affect us in this realm either positively or negatively, depending on how Divine the mind is and where each placement corresponds.

The Word "Arts" would equate to one's self-expression of skill, beauty, and creativity. Mankind is here to create, which is the beauty of life and love. This life and Love consist of both perspectives of chaos and peace. Once a man realizes his innate nature and fortifies that creativity and light energy within, harmony can take place. That does not mean we don't fortify the darkness, which is equally important. Perhaps that is one of the most important aspects of this word. I speak unto you an allegory, for there is another meaning behind the literal sense. You see, what we know as the word "Martial" is shown to us in the Chinese character "MU or WU." This means stopping fighting or putting down weapons. The first action is never to dissolve or tear down but to build and produce. The master mind is able to comprehend through philosophies of ancient combat and, in some cases, end conflict in peace without bloodshed. That is to say, in the name of the true occult meaning, whether good or bad, we realize that control of emotional faculties in terms of the essence of man shall determine his will and his creation. As it is said, Man has free will and a choice. Nature and the innate potential within man allow him absolute autonomy, as we read in the secret teachings of all ages: "Nature permits man to do anything he desires; He is limited only by his own laws and customs." Thus, we find that the word "Martial Arts" can be translated as "ending conflict skillfully." The emotional content within man can be his deliverer or his captor. For example, the biblical law of the Hebrews teaches us the concept of an eye for an eye. I know we have all heard of this being one of the "old wise sayings," but what's interesting is the savior had power over the five elements and understood the occult things, and still decided not to reciprocate the same energy received from blinded people.

According to the ancient legends in the apocryphal text, upon graduation from the mystery school, an initiate (that being Jesus or any of the masters who accomplished this task) was able to harness the power of raising the dead. This power is one of the most ancient secrets, which is very interesting because, according to the tablets of Enki, Only the highest gods would be privy to the power of raising the dead. "Ptah to RA all manner of the MEs gave. What do I know that you do not know? The father, his son, asked. Then, in all manner of knowledge, except that of the dead, reviving to RA, he gave." Ptah, being an Egyptian name of Lord Enki, meaning "The Developer." You see, the kung fu of mind is something history and the world have known before and have now forgotten. It's safe to say ending conflict skillfully could easily be something more practical in a world full of mystics and artists. Physical Fighting does not need to be involved in ending a conflict. The knowledge of words and communication, managing one's emotions or Alchemy, using intuition, and understanding vibrations (aura) should first be used. However, if one insists on escalating, we go back to the origin of the word and its literal meaning. Thus, ending anything skillfully can be graceful in terms of divine peace but also ungainly in terms of divine War. You see, Anything Can be KungFu, but Not Everything can be Martial Arts.

Throughout the years, Kung Fu and martial arts have been thought of as a way to fight. The common person has only the mind to see the literal and only the will to instruct the physical to his best abilities and utmost knowledge. Whether in the name (in this sense, the act or work produced) of Good or Evil, to serve one's master, the primary (Good) serves in love, kingship, defense, and justice; thus, Christ made manifest, polarized in the heavens. The latter (evil), which in the name of their biding causes carnal interpretations of men with a lack of cosmic nature using principles of electric thought. These vibrate at a much denser frequency. Hence why, Bruce Lee stated in his iconic interview on the Pierre Breton Show in 1971, "Honestly expressing yourself...it is very difficult to do, I can make all kind of phony things you see what I mean, blinded by it or I can show you some really fancy movement, but to express oneself honestly...Now that, my friend, is very hard to do." Likewise, Manly P. Hall quotes an excerpt in his secret teachings of all ages from one man who is said to be the first philosopher, the great master Pythagoras: "The world is herein warned that it should not attempt to interpret the mysteries of god and secret sciences without spiritual and intellectual illumination." To understand martial arts and kung fu from an unfamiliar perspective and view it from its original cosmic origin, we must open Pandora's box. Most people believe that it is all a show, just some fancy moves they see in an old Asiatic movie, with high flying kicks, soaring jumps, running on the ears of corn, or even sailing across an open body of water with just your feet. Entertaining, yes, but is it true?

Science has proven over ten years ago the innate psychic powers of man. A professor of psychology, Daryl Ben, conducted a study with over 1000 participants over an 8-year span. He tested the various forms of ESP or Psi and precognition. This is the unexplained process of information or energy transfer. Upon conclusion of these studies, he was asked if he could find any methodological flaws in one PSI researcher's successful extra-sensory perception studies- and he could not. His studies proved that the physiology of man can anticipate an upcoming event even though your conscious self might not. (see the Cornell chronicle written by George Lower) I can testify to such an experience, for in my own life, I am a witness, but what does psychic ability or energy transfer have to do with martial arts? How does this link with the perspective of modern martial arts movies? Well, chi manipulation and foresight are gifts of the illumined masters. The sages and grandmasters were always in tune with higher forces, knew things before they happened, and could act before they needed to. Written in the secret teachings of all ages, we find that this study conducted by the professor is corroborated by the sages of old. "For all things are in us psychically, and through this, we are naturally capable of knowing all things. By exciting the powers and the images of wholes which we contain." Ancient legends written on papyrus show magnificent magical miracles being completed by ordinary men. Being that of flesh and blood. The ancient Brahmin yogis and Shaolin masters have been known to energetically manipulate their bodies, putting in question the laws of physics attributed to this material realm. Science also proves what the sages have been telling us for hundreds of years. Your mind can alter your reality. According to scientists, every situation or event, past, present, or future, becomes what your brain defines it to be. In this way, your experience of reality is your own creation. Your brain physically responds by reinforcing neutral connections that coincide with your predominant, habitual thinking. This is a concept called Neuroplasticity and corresponds with the biblical teachings of the sages who speak of the secret power inside the mind of man by stating this famous quote: as a man thinketh, so is he. In other words, how he thinks mirrors his reality, and we have the power to change our reality through, learning something new with repetition and time from inside our brains to outside our bodies.

Modern Society, with the backing of Western Christendom, believes things like meditation, Hand Mudras, Chanting, frequency, energy, vibrations, etc, are evil practices and should by all means not be a part of the ascension teachings of the enlightened soul. This stance on the subject, while widely accepted, shows the lack of esoteric knowledge that the world is able to comprehend. Throughout many of the ancient texts and records of cultures, many of these practices are utilized for the utmost spiritual experiences that the average human hasn't even begun to Fathom. Men who have been counted as worthy in ancient times and now even during our age have unlocked the occult spiritual ability behind Martial Arts and, while doing so, ascend to the realm of the Gods. Great men throughout history and of modern times were and are using it as a way to protect, defend, and preserve life, but sadly, many have used these principles to cultivate the lowest form of energy and vibration. They have attached themselves to the logic and ego of the lowest man, causing unjust Death, murder, and hate, ultimately personifying chaos. Therefore, we are in a never-ending pendulum, a dance back and forth between good and evil, the spiritual greater world, and the lesser 3D world.

According to the ancient tablets, the constellation reveals peace or chaos in the world of men. It's all written in the stars. A time of peace must be followed by a time of chaos. "By the twelve constellation signs were the heavens divided, to them with his left hand Galzu pointed. From the Bull to the Ram Galzu, his pointing shifted; three times, he repeated the pointing. Then, in a dream vision, Galzu spoke up and said to Enlil: The righteous time of benevolence and peace by evildoing and bloodshed will be followed. In three celestial portions, the Ram of Marduk, the bull of Enlil, will replace one who, himself as supreme god, has declared supremacy on Earth and will seize it. A calamity as has never before occurred, by fate's decree, will happen. A time of peace must be followed by a time of chaos." Quoted from the lost book of Enki. This correlates to the 5th universal law of hermetic philosophy, The principle of rhythm. "Everything flows out and in; everything has its tides, and all things rise and fall; the pendulum swings manifest in everything. The measure of the swing to the right is the measure of the swing to the left." (See the Kybalion by the three initiates) One may ask to comprehend the meaning of fighting to save and defend lives or fighting to waste and end lives. This is a plausible query due to the fact that according to natural law, there is the choice to separate infinite light (meaning to take life) from temporal matter. My response is this: the vital energy is expelled from the vessel at the voluntary or involuntary revelation of a life cycle. Wether it is destiny or fate. Mankind was not always aware of this in the early stages of humanity, according to many ancient texts and legends, but we were acclimated very quickly when the first murder was recorded. This permanent choice must be held to the upmost importance. In no way, shape, or form am I saying that fighting for divine Peace and liberty is a bad thing? In fact, there is a Law of common cosmic Trogoautoegocratic, which states coherently two fundamental basic factors: to swallow or be swallowed or the reciprocal nourishment of all organisms. In the name of truth, this is the law of nature and of life, which will not and cannot fail. The weaker will always succumb to the stronger. So, in a dimension where practicality and originality rarely radiate, we can expect division, diversion, and dissension from an environmental basis, and we also can see the dogmatic animalistic nature of men who will not spare any being before themselves, especially if that man is over-religiously motivated. It is my belief that to truly and deeply understand what martial arts is, you will need to inner stand it from a harmonic, soulful aspect.

Furthermore, this philosophy isn't for just one person, nation, or creed. This idea is one. Correspondingly, Moses, the initiate and holy warlock, quoted from the words of the god of Israel himself, the mighty I am that I am "Hear oh Israel the lord our god is one" (See the writings of Deuteronomy). This idea isn't solely of this material plane. The heavenly body, referred to as the Macrocosm, corresponds directly with the Earthly body beneath, which is referred to as the Microcosm. From the body above, we learn the body beneath; from the body beneath, we must learn the body without; from the body without, we must learn the body within; from the body within, we must rise and be resurrected through the right hand or spiritual mind. The great Philosophers agree that we must all rise with reason in order to truly walk in the power of light. The result is the merging of heaven and earth. These thoughts and ideas go back to the furthest of civilizations, captivating even the most remote societies. Even beyond that, the art has been mastered and fortified by none other than the Gods and Goddesses who operate in the Realms above and below our physical plane. You will find that even the Gods repent and learn as life flows.

In some schools of thought, what we know now as martial arts is nothing, but the lesser knowledge taught to man through the first generations of this world by deities or fallen angels. This Lesser knowledge brought carnal desires and a carnal personification of the art. This is not solely due to the profundity of the wisdom learned because we know knowledge is neither good nor evil; rather, it is a neutral energy. This means the principles of both polarities can be expressed from the same soul or individual. We all have a choice on how we will use the energy inside of us. Aliens, the Anunnaki, Enki and Enlil, the watchers, fallen Angels, the Demiurge, and Archons have many names and are known throughout all cultures and customs. These beings govern higher realms of thought; they constitute different frequencies and vibrations, and regardless of what we call them, they originate from the same source that we come from, which is Light. All these things and much more will go into this. From this moment on, I will use the term "Martial Arts" solely as the subject of discussion because we now know the difference between the two closely related terms, with the primary being the center point. With this information provided, I only ask that you listen to this prospective presented and try to absorb the spirit behind each and everything we do in life. It ALL HAS A BEGINNING.

CH.3
THE LESSER KNOWLEDGE | |

FIGHTING TO ACHIEVE POWER WILL GET YOU DESTROYED BY THE SAME POWER YOU SEEK. IF THE FIGHT IS TO OBTAIN WISDOM AND SKILLS, THIS GIVES YOU THE BALANCE BETWEEN MIND, SPIRIT, AND BODY.

The secrets of God seem to have been a pursuit of man since the dawn of time. The deep, dark caverns of infinite knowledge are yet to be explored through the eyes of the awakened. There is a legend of wisdom concerning the Anunnaki. A name that means those who from the heavens fell, have had their place among ancient folklore and religious texts through the ages of man. Sons of Anu they have been called in many of the ancient papyrus. A more modern term is the fallen angels or the watchers, referenced in the book of Enoch and in the King James Version of the modern Bible. Some theologians and researchers use the word Alien, which corresponds with the Hebrew word Elohim, one of the earliest languages in the world. In my opinion, one of the most popular terms to identify these beings is that of extra-terrestrials made popular through sci-fi and propagandized campaigns in today's secular society, as well as the entertainment industry. If we reference legends that predate the Old Testament, we can find these strange beings and clearly identify what or maybe who they are. Interestingly, in the ancient Sumer legends of Mesopotamia, we find these stories deep in the earth inscribed on clay tablets. Eloquently preserved to keep the ancient history remembered and intact. In addition to this fact, we can also find numerous archeological sites in various locations, hieroglyphs in some of the most ancient groves and places of worship, and ancient historical wonders of the world erected in symbolism, each having a hidden origin while revealing a telling story to the illumined informed. The hieroglyphs on the walls of ancient pyramids and cuneiform earthen clay tablets tell of a group of beings descending on Earth and manipulating the existing hominids on the planet. Not only were these people manipulated, but they were also cross-spliced, genetically tampered with, and completely cultivated. Although there are many translations of these tablets throughout history, according to the world's top theologians and scholars, through careful study and research, these stories closely correlate or are, in fact, the same stories written in the Bible. They are referenced in the book of Enoch and many other ancient records of pre-existing cultures. These modern enlightened souls, we have termed this "Synchronizations." Being able to recognize the code. In my opinion, one of the most interesting stories concerning the

Annunaki is the story of the pre-flood world and the gods who shaped humanity as we know it.

Written in the book of Enoch, God reveals to the enlightened sage the secrets of all, and while God did not allow Enoch to release all the cosmic secrets, he was able to give the world of men just enough to create those who thirst for more. During his exploits, Enoch is shown by the heavenly angels the armies of heaven! Myriads and myriads of different powerful beings are lined in order of rank. "In the middle of heaven, I saw armed troops, worshipping the lord with tympani and pipes and unceasing voices." (See the 2nd book of Enoch) Now, ask yourself, why would God need armed angels? I would assume anything remotely threatening god himself has made, so there would be no need, right? What we have uncovered has brought the words of this book to life. The great Enoch was taken many times throughout his life. According to the text, God bids Enoch to transport a message to the Watchers: "You have been in heaven, but all the mysteries had not yet been revealed to you, and you knew worthless ones. And these in the hardness of your hearts you have made known to the women. And through the mysteries, women and men work much evil on the earth." (See the 1st book of Enoch). I have coined this, "The Lesser knowledge" in terms of how men perceive the mystery and how they understood its secrets. Some may ask why a distinction is made. Well, I believe, in fact, that all knowledge is central and key to life experience; however, through ignorance, knowledge is easily distorted. Enoch was an initiate of the highest order. As legends have it, his physical flesh never expired. He was taught the battle of duality, which is good vs evil. Right vs left, good knowledge vs bad knowledge. The great Enoch knew this paradigm was an illusion and that only perspective, thought, word, and action could lead to one of these two degrees of good and evil. The mystic Manly P. Hall states, "God also set the opposites against each other: the good against the evil, and the evil against the good. Good proceeds from good, Evil from evil; the good purifies the bad, the bad the good. The good is reserved for the good, and the evil for the wicked." These polarities are not different entities but rather distinct aspects of the same pole. Manly P. Hall also goes on to state, "There are three of which each standby itself: One is in the affirmative (filled with good), one is in the negative (filled with evil), and the third equilibrates them." (see the secret teachings of all ages). The equilibrium is the balancing. A harmonic factor between the two aspects of the same pole. You see, the power of perspective is an important aspect here. As we dig deeper into what this lesser knowledge is, we go to another important scripture in the text to give us a clue.

Referenced from the enlighten Enoch, "and Azazel taught men to make swords and knives and shields and make known to them the metals of the earth and the art of working them, and bracelets and ornaments, and the use of Antimony, and the beautifying of eyelids, and all kinds of costly stones, and all the coloring tinctures." From this excerpt, I believe we get a clue as to what this lesser knowledge entails. It Is the arts of warfare, economic, sensual, mental, and societal dominance. This knowledge would have the power to control and govern all the ignorant inhabitants on earth at that time. We also see the culmination of this earth realm wisdom, which could raise the inhabitants who received this knowledge to a new estate. The degree of elevation depends upon what type of people would receive it. As we read the ancient text, it plainly points to the theory that because of this lesser knowledge the watchers disseminated to men and women, they have worked evil against God. But is this the direction the holy scribe Enoch wanted to portray to the future generations of the world? Without the modern sciences that were taught to men and women, the world would not have advanced in the manner it has today. Though the world seems to be in disarray, there is the same amount of beauty and order keeping the world balanced. Only perspective and the willingness to expand would allow one to see through this illusion. When we read further in the text, it seems that what humans were taught was only the literal sense from which corruption can only be yielded. They were not taught the secret aspects of the sciences they learned, which would yield harmony. Written in allegory, the sword, shield, and knives are likened to military conquests over the entire earth or even angelic conquests because as we search through history, one can truly find the battle of the gods and their orchestration throughout mankind. The metals of the earth contain an energetic impulse measured within and without the world around us. This knowledge seemed to be used for the corruption of magic internally and externally, as well as the knowledge of the periodic table, which consists of all the known elements and technological applications. Bracelets and ornaments with the use of antimony, a symbol of physical worth, royalty, and biological chemical attraction. The beautifying of eyelids, to the unlearned promoted immorality while portraying illusion, and the costly stones with coloring tinctures are the sum of all, the ultimate greed of man.

As we begin to understand how this concept corresponds with not only martial arts and its origins but also spirituality and the soul truths it holds, one would need to remember that each legend consists of viewpoints and perspectives that are accompanied by its theology through individual cultures. In other words, each legend speaks of the same thing in separate ways, and it is key for you to understand this, as one perspective is but a piece of the spiritual universal puzzle. Therefore, it is my belief that in order to have a complete picture, we must check all sources of the same story. The corruption of humankind was not solely due to lesser knowledge. Why? Knowledge does not have a conscience and does not originate in duality, for it is neither good nor evil. Rather, it is a neutral energy. It is the decisions from the illumination of knowledge that qualifies character. Man only knows what he has been taught and will forever be ensnared unless awakened to his identity and power. "Action is our relationship to everything. Action is not a matter of right or wrong. It is only when action is partial that there is a right and a wrong. Do not let your attention be arrested! Transcend dualistic comprehension of a situation." (Quoted from the Tao of Jeet Kune Do)

Let's look at another exert referenced from the book of Enoch: "And the third was named Gadreel, It is he who showed the children of men the blows of death, and he led astray eve and showed the weapons of death and the shield and the coat of mail, and the sword for battle, and all the weapons of death to the children of men." In Terms of Conflict, let us first look at the origin of the sword. The sword is said to have been developed during the Bronze Age, evolving from the dagger. The earliest specimens date to about 1600 bc. The first weapons that can be described as swords date to around 3300 BC. Before the evolution of the dagger to the sword, tools like this were already in use by the gods. As it is written in the books of Genesis, "So he drove out the man, and he placed at the east of the garden of Eden cherubim, and a flaming sword which turned every way, to keep the way of the tree of life" This would indicate that not only did the angels keep high-grade weaponry, but that warfare was nothing new to such a being. The so-called fallen angels knew of all that was needed in order to create these weapons, and they also knew exactly how to train a man to do so. This is roughly five to six thousand years before the book of Enoch was said to be written. The Mesniu (Metal people) were according to Egyptain traditions, the first men ever to have been armed by the gods with weapons made of metal or "divine iron". These men were also the first to be enlisted by a god to fight in the wars between the gods. (See the wars of gods and men by Zechariah Sitchins) There is a movie called The Eternals, which shows the gods being sent to Earth with the purpose of excelling in the development of mankind. This movie aligns with ancient texts and history in that very aspect. These weapons are tools that are still in use to this very day. You see, all legends have some truth in them.

The blows of death taught to men by the supernatural gods signify a pearl of ancient worldly wisdom only a creator would know of his creation. Having the intelligence of anatomy can form power on many levels. The blows of death would eventually transform into a secret art only master's could receive. In and on the human body, there are specific points of attack, and with the right velocity, a man can be instantly harmed. There is an ancient Chinese concept known to the wise sages as Dim Mak, which translates to press Artery. This is a secret body of knowledge with techniques that attack pressure points and meridians. It is said to incapacitate at once or even cause delayed death to an opponent. These locations on the body are mostly points in between the main extremities. For example, the location between the knee and the hip joint on the leg is what you call a point of pain. A well-placed attack with enough force would severely damage an opponent. Here is another example: the location between the top of the neck and the collar bone is also a pain point. A well-placed attack here can instantly kill your opponent. According to the account in Enoch, the fallen angels felt it was important for a man to understand these pain points, and through this knowledge, much bloodshed spread through the ages. Interestingly, little scientific or historical evidence exists for such a martial art, but legends written in ancient texts prove otherwise. There are also many demonstrations of different versions of this technique shown to us in movies through Hollywood or even on television. Ty Lee, a fire nation warrior maiden from Avatar: The Last Air Bender, displays her skills using this god style very eloquently. Just as simple as this can be used for war, this knowledge can also be used in a positive way, for pressure points and meridians are energetic centers that can also be used to heal. This knowledge is also said to be traced to a Chinese medicine, that is called acupuncture. These blows of death are widely considered a legend in most circles; however, to the truly informed and those who are aware of anatomy, this is an ancient secret of science and combat. When we think in terms of Warfare, fighting styles, and the blows of death, in any situation where this is needed, one has many gates by which the conflict can be halted. These gates are entry points on the body where energy can penetrate, causing maximum in-balance in mind and body. It does not matter which of the gates are first accessed or in which order. For example, a blast of energy in the form of any physical or psychic attack can disrupt and disable vital energy centers.

The knowledge of these things was taught to ancient man with the intent to shelter the masses from its nectar of the soul truths within. With the age of technology, these things are easily researched; however, some still attest to the fact that hidden deep within the elite are the true eternal secrets. The origins of the weapons of death are not just swords, shields, and knives but also weapons of mass destruction. Manipulation of vital energy for detrimental use. Technology that is much more advanced is now posted and immortalized on hieroglyphs throughout the earth. It seems fiction has become reality. As philosophic martial artists, we aspire to seek all knowledge. The lesser knowledge truly only covers the base value of what we actually could become when we truly delve into the secrets.

CH.4
MIND, CREATION, AND SELF-EXPRESSION | |

A wise soul is like a painter creating a horizon. The painter does not only use one color. Instead, he blends and adapts, using and adding new colors to create his desired idea.

In the Beginning, God created the heavens and the earth, and God said, "Let there be light." Quoted from the King James bible, there are so many perspectives and interpretations of this statement from a religious point of view, and in my educated opinion, this quote is one of the most interesting pieces of sacred text out there. This leads us to this question: what is that light from the beginning, and what was born from it? Science reveals a fact that has been a part of the cosmic foundation since the creation of the temporal world. The advent of matter, i.e., the material world we live in, is, in fact, condensed light down to every particle, atom, and wave. There is a quantum mechanics theory called the "Copenhagen interpretation," which states that an object, when observed, is forced to take one state or another. Depending on the object. These structures and buildings that appear physical and solid only appear to be according to vibratory rate and frequency. When a person is not around to observe these condensed atoms, they don't exist or they relay back to there primary state, which is waves and energy. As soon as a conscious observer interacts with these objects, they condense into solid visible matter. Our brains and the universe co-actively create our environment. "All things that can be seen by human eyes are manifests of aught and naught

53

and must so pass away. The things we see are but reflexes just appearing, while the ethers vibrate so and so, and when conditions change, they disappear." (see the Aquarian gospel of Jesus the Christ). We all have heard of the great mind and scientist Albert Einstein and his theoretical equation of $E=mc2$, which states that all mass is condensed energy and in its purest form, energy is light. Well, everything in our material realm is actually fractals of energy from the creative light mentioned in the King James Bible. What is very interesting is that even our thoughts are light alongside other forms of energy we cannot see. We will cover this in another chapter. Even though everything seems to be at rest, each and every physical and non-physical substance moves at a vibratory rate. The third hermetic law and universal principle of vibration states that all things, both physical matter and spiritual energy, hold a certain vibration and are in constant motion. (See the Kyballion). Basic science teaches us that atoms are in constant motion, just as the universe itself is. For example, our heart, as it beats, gives off a certain vibration depending on our emotional state, and from our emotional state combined with the thoughts we think and the five sense observatories of our anatomy, we create this light matrix called reality 3D.

You see, what we call God is interpreted by the great philosophers, mystics, and sages as the creative force from which all things originate. That force is a supreme being called the mind. As stated in the secret teachings of all ages, "The supreme being- the mind- male and female, brought forth the word, and the word suspended between light and darkness was delivered of another mind called the workman, the master builder, or the maker of all things" In the grand scheme of all religions we have the aspect of Gender. This is also a universal law found in the Kyballion. Divine male and Divine female bring life and love, which is creation; this contains all aspects of matter and spirit matter. He goes on to state in this wonderful work, "Thy god am the light, and the mind which was before the substance was divided from spirit and darkness from light." Contained in that force was the complete and absolute essence of every Idea, which are thought forms, every atom, photon, electron, and neutron, all plant and animal life with their corresponding planes and corpuscles, and even the Homo-Sapien. The heavens aligned their cosmic portals and opened their energetic gates for light to decent into this realm, which in turn corresponds with the spirit of God hovering over the celestial waters called the face of the deep.

In the ancient books of the Hebrews, the demigod Enoch, who was translated and transmuted into one of the highest angels in the heavens according to the ancient texts, stated an idea perceived from the heavens that all of the lowest things of this reality were contained in spirit matter, solid, dense and great darkness. "And called out a second time into the very lowest things, and I said Let one of the invisible things come out visibly solid, and Arkham came out (the Lower foundation) solid, and heavy, and very black, and I said open yourself Arkham and let what is born from you become visible. And he disintegrated himself. There came out an age, dark, very large, carrying the creation of all the lower things, and I saw how good it was." As we see here, even the apparent darkness is a form of good. He then goes on to state that light, which came from the highest and brightest components of cosmic thought, contained all from which the heavenly circuits are manifested. Thus, the invisible nonphysical things are also called the Cosmophysical things. "And I command the highest things; let one of the invisible things descend visibly! And Adoil (the Upper foundation) descended, which was extremely large. And I looked at him, and behold, in his belly, he had a great light. And I said to him. Disintegrate yourself, Adoil, and let what is born from you become visible; he disintegrated himself, and there came out a very great light. And I was in the midst of that great light, and light out of light is carried thus, and the great age came out, and it revealed all of the creation which I had thought up to create, and I saw how good it was."(see the writings of 2 Enoch Pseudepigrapha) Therefore, eternal light and eternal darkness, the two polarities from which all things begin, had their origin together, and their origins are in the invisible and manifest here in the physical whether we see them or not. This text brings a new ideological revelation to the understanding that these ages, yet different in ratio, are but the same in propensity to natural forces. Instead of opposition, they, in fact, are in harmony, balancing the everlasting space of the cosmos.

Similar to the divisions of seasons and time, there is an eternal barrier embedded in its codes for no deviation; correspondingly, there is a divisional barrier between each plane of consciousness. Some wise men call these divisions densities, paradises, or maybe even heavens. Whatever you choose to call it, these realities are worlds within themselves, completely layered on top of the material reality we are currently experiencing. Understanding this, by faith, that is, with an inherent trust and enduring confidence in the power, wisdom, and goodness of God, we understand that the worlds (universe, ages) were framed and created (formed, put in order, and equipped for their intended purpose) by the word of God so that what is seen was not made out of things which are visible. (See the writings to the Hebrews) According to the Kabbalist's school of thought, this is explained in terms of divisions, Rings, or barriers, "Each ring includes within its own nature all the rings within itself. Thus, the primitive dot (which is the source or primordial point of energy) controls and contains all rings which it encloses, all of this partaking of its own nature in varying degrees according to their respective dignities." In the ancient esoterica of the Hebrew mystery schools, the sephiroth tree is comprised of 9 divisions or worlds with different aspects or angles of light emanating their energies to man. Let's take a look at the sephiroth in the form of the universe from Maurice's Indian Antiquities. "Comprised of nine spheres, the sephrioth is superimposed, decreasing in size, as they decrease in power and dignity. Thus, the crown is the greatest and all-inclusive, and the kingdom that represents the physical universe is the smallest and least important." (See the secret teachings of all ages) In biblical cosmetology, it's called the firmament, which binds mankind and aliens alike to the earth. Some schools of thought believe the firmament is a barrier that divides the world from the world, with the capacity to travel through gates or portals via the stars embedded in it but never crack the dome in the sky.

The ancients speak of seven firmaments with which all things are encompassed, and the ALL father being founded at the top on his throne, with light stretched out as far as the eye could see. This is also recorded in second Enoch. It is said that there is nothing higher than light besides nothing itself; likewise, there is nothing lower than darkness but nothing itself. "And I placed for myself a throne and sat down on it. And then to the light I spoke, you go up higher than the throne and be solidified much higher than the throne and become the foundation for the highest things. And there is nothing higher than the light except nothing itself." Enoch also wrote down the same statement for the lower foundation, "and I told him (Arkhas, the lower foundation) to come down low and become solid! And become the foundation for the lowest things. And it came about, and he came down and became solid, and he became the foundation for the lowest things. There is nothing lower than darkness but nothing itself." (See 2nd Enoch Pseudepigrapha) Some text goes so far as to say there are ten heavens or dimensional spaces where the emanations of God are manifest, but that's a conversation for another time. (Please see the writings of the ancient Hebrews.) Interestingly enough, science now proves the validity of mankind being multidimensional beings and having a psychic relationship between nonphysical dimensions. Not to mention, the sages all knew that everything is psychic in man. Proclus, in his first book on the Theology of Plato, states concerning the soul, "When, however, she proceeds into her interior recesses and into the septum as it were of the soul, she perceives it with her eyes closed (without the aid of the lower mind) the genus of the gods and the unities of beings. For all things are in us psychically, and through this, we are naturally capable of knowing all things, by exciting the powers and the images of wholes which we contain." A study published in Frontiers in Computational Neuroscience reveals that the human brain creates neural structures and operates in up to 11 dimensions, the study was conducted by the "blue brain project". Very interesting stuff! Now, let's get back to the most generous gift of light from the beginning of creation.

The descent of light is one of God's greatest self-expressions, in my opinion. Without light, this realm would be out of balance and could not exist. Indeed, inside the primordial darkness of creation, light is shone. Likewise, the body is a brilliant electromagnetic energy expressing itself in the threefold manner of light and radiance while creating life. The greater light or the sun, which all saviors are based upon, is the everlasting savior above, giving warmth and life to all of nature. This fact is but the cornerstone of all existence, wisdom, and knowledge. Here entails the secret meaning of as above so below. Embedded in that light was the energy for everything, and only when you correspond with your calling from the heavens in authenticity to you, with the perfecting of the three-fold nature of man, anatomically, spiritually, and mentally, then can you express yourself truly. The Philosophers believe "spirituality does not make men righteous nor rational, but rather righteousness and rationalism will make men spiritual." (Quoted from the Secret teachings of all ages.) If one is taught to mimic the expression of another, he cannot truly become divine. He can climb, but only to a point, then one becomes un-fruitful or stagnant. When there is not growth within the soul of a called being, it will produce mental, emotional, and physical digression. Man becomes complacent, and some will choose to lay eternally in their folly.

Through decoding myself and my environment, the following became apparent to me. I believe in the preservation of life, but what life are we talking about? In my opinion, the life we are programmed to accept is against the natural ascension of self-expression in any individual. A programmed mind contains within itself a hindered soul and spirit. Which in turn buries our true power, destroys our reason, and decimates our god given will. This is why we have always heard of the sages and enlightened masters of old speaking about a renewal of mind. More recently, we reference the parable of the Hebrew sage Jesus while speaking with the pharisee Nicodemous, "Except a man be born of water and the spirit," A beautiful mystic parable. "Astronomically water, according to William Herschel, pouring from the urn of Aquarius under the name of "the waters of eternal life" appears much in symbolism." (See the secret teachings of all ages by Manly P. Hall) These same waters appear to be the waters mentioned in the books of Adam and Eve, which would water the entire garden and flow from the eternal source itself. These particular waters were able to rejuvenate life back into Adam after apparent multiple suicide attempts. (These suicides are found written in the books of Adam and Eve.) You see, the water baptism esoterically correlates to raising the cosmic fire in the center of man's being, thus bringing him to a divine degree of purity. This is because the spinal cord is the main source of communication between the body and the brain. This process requires physical renewal, but more on a spiritual level, we begin to gain its secrets and wisdom. Some may ask, what exactly are we referring to here, and why does this matter? Well, with proper exegesis of the ancient text, we find there is a symbolic meaning to many, if not all of the rituals and rites written in scripture, for all things, are done symbolically according to the Apostles of Jesus themselves. "I held firmly this one thing in my mind that the lord contrived all things symbolically and as a dispensation toward men for their conversion and salvation" (see the Gnostic Acts of Apostles).

Now, Let's look at faith; it is said that faith is the substance of things hoped for, the evidence of things not seen. (See the writings to the Hebrews) This has become something not short of Marvel or fairy tales because in the ancient texts, when we hear of faith, there is always a magical tendency towards its completion. Even when it comes to moving mountains, raising the dead, or calming the tempest seas and winds, there is a fractal of faith that is said to be so powerful, one would only need a mustard seed measurement. It is said by once great souls something similar to this. Whenever you see a legend, you can be sure that if you go to the very bottom of things, YOU WILL FIND HISTORY. (see the quotes of Auguste Vallet de Viriville) I've come to find that true faith (not the "faith" we are accustomed to) is, in fact, a sacred energy, frequency, and vibration. I'm not referring to the act of "praying, begging, and hoping" planes of thought we were taught in churches, masques, and cathedrals. I'm talking about the divine sacred energy that complements the spirit, soul, and body and which is a part of every being. This faith teaches us to be engulfed with an aura as if what we declared has already happened. I'm referring to the true occult knowledge of subconscious faith.

Believe it or not, this information was actually given to us in the ancient version of the Gospels and taught to the earliest

Christians before extensive collusion of the holy scriptures. Compliments of one of the great sages of our time, Greg Brendan, with his studies on historical theology and biblical text, in order to find this ancient passage, we would need to go into a different version of the modern-day biblical text, and by doing so, we find true subconscious faith written off in the Aramaic translation of the earliest versions of the King James Bible. "All things that you ask straightly directly from inside my name (character) you will be given. So far, you have not done this. Ask without hidden motive and be surrounded by your answer; be enveloped by what you desire that your gladness may be full." Let's stop and imagine how different the world would be if the complete understanding of faith and prayer were taught to the masses. This is just one example of many of the hidden exerts cloaked throughout the ages, and through the ancient political and religious structures of men, records that would remotely help conclude the entire story of the soul and its power with this mundane 3D reality and ultimately free the masses would be taken away for thousands of years.

What do scriptures have to do with martial arts? Why is this important? Lastly, what is the correlation between faith and art? Well, if faith is actually an energy that we must harness subconsciously in order to physically move mountains, that very statement shakes the martial arts community to its core. Just imagine the true spirit of martial arts being realized, the complete light of the soul and mind. Mastery of regulating chi or the divine breath subconsciously, combined with the magical properties of the DNA within each individual, would produce nothing short of a real-life anime character. According to the kyballion, men who wield these abilities have walked this earth. Harnessing the creative powers of the gods as gold transmuted from even the grossest form of mundane matter to the highest form of spirit matter! These men and women operate with those who are privileged and initiated. Theoretically, one could control the four elements at the least, but at his greatest, he shall be one with the All, which is cosmic unity without physical deterioration, the goal of all ancient mysteries. We must show how these spiritual things correspond with martial arts because spirit is the main force used in this school of thought. Without spirit, art is nothing but a tangible shell of the substantial reality. Vain and coherently temporal is the art that doesn't have life and breath.

The word Martial to the esteemed is also a dark saying or many-faced allegory as the root word links to war, and its true essence being that of peace, two components of the same pole and two variations of the same aspect, just different degrees. The soul cannot completely merge with the ALL until the collective conscious growth of all the universe is accomplished, but you can come very, very close as any ascended master who walked this plane. Thoth, in his emerald tablets, referenced man having the ability to master space-time, and with certain meditation practices, out-of-body experiences can happen at will, with unlimited access to the cosmos through eternal corners of light. Merging heaven and earth, sealed like the signet ring of God given to the great and wise grandmaster king Solomon. You see, the Spirit is divine light, and light is energy. To understand Energy, you must grasp the idea of electric Light, which is thought, creation, and awareness. This is where we get the term "I am That I AM." That, my friend, is the basis of understanding self-expression. Biblically, Mankind is the expression of God, who is the ever-expanding mind from primordial light. "Now man himself is mind, and mind is here to gain perfection by experience, and mind is often manifest in fleshy form and in the form best suited for its growth. So, the mind may manifest as worm, or bird, or beast, or man" (see the Aquarian gospel of Jesus, the Christ). Not only Mankind but all creatures of creation. "For in him we live and move and exist (that is in him we actually have our being) see the Acts of the Apostles)

The universe and dimensions are also the expressions of God. Self-expression is first developed by the study of self through meditation and by inner standing, the origin of one's Spirit, Soul, and Body, which is sometimes referred to as the lower trinity in man. Do not think of this as a religious concept due to the dogma behind the word "trinity," yet this is referring to the secrets of numerology and the power of 3, which is creation according to the Hebrew Kabbalah. It is my conclusion If a man is honest with himself and others and exercises the 7 Holy Fruits of the spirit, there are no limits In this reality or the next. In some thought groups, there are nine virtues. Each is accompanied by its opposite polarity. Peace, Gentleness, goodness (truth), kindness, patience, joy, self-control, faithfulness, and love. These things only elevate your soul and raise your consciousness. You may have heard this in the ancient text: with proper transmutation upon these mental and conscious realizations; you will not care for what you lack or care for the things of this world; you will not care for what happens to your body because this mortality has been changed to immortality, reality will be your playground. Divine love is what you disseminate, and a chaste and discipline life is what you live by, much like spontaneous movement from hearing your favorite song or the joy your face expresses when you taste delectable food. These little human tendencies are what make us each different yet somehow connect us all the same. Subconsciously, the true essence of who we are will manifest, causing reality to express itself honestly in your life. When a soul studies any form of martial arts, he must accept wisdom with an open heart and mind. Seeing the world through the eye of a keyhole cuts off the knowledge that may piece in the entire puzzle.

Hidden throughout the ages of time are the ancient knowledge and wisdom of old spoken to us in legends and allegories. These were copied and reiterated but with the same soul truths that will awaken the dry bones like the prophet Ezekiel spoke about. Different perceptions of the world we live in may become different avenues, but like the rays from the sun, they all stem from the same source and originate in that archetype. A great example I can provide you with is the way which was made straight by the mystic harbinger or the consecration of the holy Hebrew law by way of Moses, which could ultimately lead to the same destination through different viewpoints in each individual reality. As students of law, art, and spirituality, we begin to unlock a full-circle comprehension of a complex law called relativity. This law allows us to decisively achieve perspective by comparing one to the other, both yielding different experiences. Through travel, I have come to realize that perspective and expression of self depend on a soul's ability to cope with its material life, including its surroundings, transmuting dark, which are the attributes we don't like, into light. Light is the spark that cannot be hidden. It's time that we talk about the concept of the "Electric Idea."

CH.5
THE ELECTRIC IDEA||

POWER AND CREATION ALL COME FROM THE FORCE OF THE MENTAL PLANE

According to Physiology, there are 86 billion Neurons inter-connected to 100 trillion to quadrillion synapses that are firing messages back and forth while forming a thought inside your brain. One study suggests that these firing neurons, which are the cells that make up your brain, use about two-thirds of its total energy, which would bring insight into why mental exhaustion could deteriorate the entire body. The Neurons release brain chemicals known as neurotransmitters, which generate electrical signals from charged molecules called ions to neighboring neurons. The charged signals propagate like a wave to thousands of neurons, which leads to thought formation. In other words, our brains are Electromagnetic; the neurons inside our brains self-generate electrical light, causing illumination. Thus, different colors of light waves, from ultra-violent to red and near-infrared, are used. Concerning the concept of thought, we have fairly touched the surface level. You will find that our entire body, in totality, is an electrical magnetic system. In other words, we are energy literally. Fun fact: according to science, the human brain can generate about 23 watts of power. That is enough to power a lightbulb.

Here is an esoteric gem for those on the journey: "In the tree, there is the hard exterior, then the fluid sap, and within that is the vital essence. Matching this in man, there is his gross outer physical body, within that the blood, and in that, as we know, the pranic electricity of life." (See the writings of Alvin Boyd Kuhn:" As amazing as it sounds, we humans lack the capacity to fathom what this truly means. The same way thought patterns are formed inside our brain is the same way thought patterns are formed inside the mind of THE ALL (which we currently are, according to some schools of thought.) Oh yes, everything you can think of and everything you can imagine exists in and out of space-time. Our mind and imagination are the gates to the worlds of the universe. The same way man manifests on this plane via our intentional or unintentional thoughts and emotions is the same way THE ALL operates on the cosmic plane. In order for man to be raised to a higher level of reason, we must be wise to our current state and composition. Man must learn himself in order to learn outside of himself. The problem is that in today's society, we are not taught anything remotely important about our inner nature, nor how we correspond to this reality. So, we stay day after day, life after life, age after age, in the same repetitive cycle. Stuck in the pendulum swing of karma and emotion. With the lack of comprehension of such forces, we are forever hindered and withheld from our true, powerful purpose.

To all seeking students of force and light, please remember the ancient hermetic axiom "As above, so below." This teaches an infallible fact that all life adheres to, whether they are privy to it or not. The human body is a universe inside of an even bigger and more complex universe; the brain itself is said to have the same number of neurons in it as the number of stars in the Milky Way. Some might even say the galaxies and stars are the brain of God. Again, here, we must remember what we have learned in relation to 360 substantial realities. That everything is in the mind of God. In the same manner, man generates thoughts and inspirational ideas on the mental plane, and they manifest here on the physical plane; God itself generates thoughts that manifest on all planes. Let's look into the ancient teachings of the three initiates for a deeper breakdown concerning this mystery. "The Hermetic Teachings concerning the creation of the universe are that at the beginning of the creative cycle, THE ALL, in its aspect of "Being" projects its will towards the aspect of "Becoming" and the process of creation begins." This correlates to the biblical narrative of the spirit of God hovering over the face of the deep, yet it gives a more intense insight into the ALL and its state of being. This also can be seen according to the 2nd book of Enoch, which states that before anything was formed, God, source, or THE ALL, which ever you call it, was moving in the invisible circuits of the cosmos and received a thought as to a visible creation. The key word here is thought. "For before any visible things had come into existence, I, the one, moved around in the invisible things like the sun, from east to west and from west to east. But the sun has rest in itself, yet I did not find rest because everything was not yet created. And I thought up an idea to establish a foundation. To create a visible creation." However, the spiritual proceeded to the physical, but the physical is the lowest foundation of all existence.

Now, the Kybalion goes on to state, "It is taught that the process consists of the lowering of vibration until a very low degree of vibratory energy is reached, at which point the grossest form of matter is manifested. This process is called the stage of involution, in which THE ALL becomes involved or wrapped up in his creation. This process is believed by the Hermeticist to have some correspondence to the mental processes of an artist, writer, or inventor, who becomes so wrapped up in his mental creation as to almost forget his own existence and who, for the time being, almost lives in his creation." The reason why this is so important is because we truly need to fathom just how every god-given attribute of man has existed energetically prior to his incarnation. We are a part of THE ALL, as THE ALL is a part of us. The Bible states that we are made in the image and likeness; hereby, we understand the ancient axiom, as above so below. For a thought or idea to be formed, a man, in his state of being, needs to deliberate within himself. Once a man assumes this act of deliberation, the mental and physical processes of the brain inaugurate the creative energies needed to establish what we call an idea. I like to call it the "electric Idea," for we have already touched base on the physical processes the brain undergoes during thought, which is just energy and light. "The ancient Hermeticists use the word meditation in describing the process of the mental creation of the universe in the mind of THE ALL, and the word contemplation is also frequently employed. The Hermetic teachings regarding the process of evolution are that THE ALL, having meditated upon the beginning of creation, having thus established the material foundations of the universe, having thought it into existence, then gradually awakens and rouses from its meditation, and in doing so starts into manifestation the process of evolution on the material, mental and spiritual planes, successively in that order." Everything originated in the mind of THE ALL, From the smallest and grossest forms of matter to the biggest and most beautiful forms of aether or spirit matter.

In any form of Art, for anything to be created, we must first set our intention from our current state, whether at rest or in motion. This is the aspect of "Being." Then, we must shift that intention to what we desire and intend. It is said that as a man thinketh, so is he. Now, this is the aspect of "Becoming," which is just a sense of being that has evolved. We have been gifted a body. This magnificent structure is comprised of three separate constitutions, yet the three are one. Did you know that the body has a total of three brains? The head brain, the heart brain, and the gut-brain. What happens when these three brains operate in unison at optimum efficiency? Interesting. Here is another fun fact about the body. Earthing or "grounding" supplies the vessel with many health benefits when connected barefoot to the earth. The earth is also electromagnetic; when the body is properly plugged in, it becomes a natural conductor. Multi-disciplinary research has revealed that electrically conductive contact of the human body with the surface of the earth produced intriguing effects on the physiology and health of man. Such effects relate to inflammation, immune responses, wound healing, and prevention and treatment of chronic inflammatory and autoimmune diseases. Very intriguing. Taking in sunlight can literally re-charge you and is known to help balance the cosmic energies in your life.

I have said this often, and I will say it again: once we as mankind can understand our bodies and treat them as life and light, then we will comprehend God, who is the universal light, which means that naturally, there is a way to correspond with nature. Therefore, doing so will enlighten our minds about carnality. The ancient text says the carnal mind is enmity against God, but the spiritual mind resurrects man from darkness to luminous. Much like the dormant brain cells that explode of light when properly energized! Harnessing the energy of esoteric faith, which we mentioned earlier, would allow control over the four elements but only with discipline. This esoteric faith correlates to the aether, the 5th element because it directly allows one with the mental capacity to bend the other four elements. The elements are archetypal powers within our minds, bringing us back within. The way the body is polluted now, modern society makes the notion of unruliness customary, which, according to one's perspectives and beliefs, would shape our outlooks on reality. We are programmed from the time of birth in fascist schools of logic; we are trained by teachers of blindness, feeding the beast of curiosity and desires. This keeps us out of balance with nature. Therefore, our consciousness will be seared with a hot iron, as it so eloquently states in the scriptures.

If you want your body to operate on the same frequency as nature, you will need to be completely in tune with Mother Earth, as she is the beauty of the entire world. If we do this, our vibration will be at a level where this realm can't do anything but bend to our electric will. Similarly, like the electricity of the mind, the body should be trained in a way that promotes harmony with its other inhabitants. We must be reborn through crucifixion and rise to a new subconscious and conscious level. Not in a religious sense, so to speak, but in a sense of self-equity and adulation. Having the components in the mind collectively communicate within the speed of light, expanding and contracting, creating friction and energy that produces "the thought" of man, which scientifically and chemically in the brain is luminous. This luminous thought then turns into "the will" of man because the body Is the vehicle used to physically manifest light by work in action. I perceive that the origin of martial arts is light and electricity in the mind of God, so the entire body of man needs to be in order to function without limits. There are three legs of infinity: Energy, frequency, and vibration. These govern realities. The spirit, the soul, and the body are components of the lower things, which, when managed correctly, make the body full of light, and that light is power and energy. Now, concerning Biblical Theology, the premise is on earth as it is in heaven. In the Occult things, they say as Above, so Below. In the metaphysical, they have said as within so without. So, it's safe to say to understand Man, the microcosm, is to get a glimpse of God, the macrocosm, and by doing so, seeing the face of god, becoming what the masters have said, " I and my father are one." The light that was present in the beginning contained everything this universe consists of, even you. Each dimension, every principality, and every power came from the light, which, prior to creation, was the thoughts of God. Here lies the occult wisdom of Martial Arts.

CH.6
THE TEMPLE, THE SOUL, THE SPIRIT||

VAIN AND COHERENTLY TEMPORAL IS THE ART THAT DOESN'T HAVE LIFE AND BREATH

There are three main factors that correspond to the collective balance of Mankind. The first is the physical temple, body, or avatar, which is the vessel the soul is given to experience life. The five sense observatories are connected tightly to this plane, allowing the entity within to feed its systems with the knowledge and wisdom needed for growth gained from experience and trial. According to religious exegesis, the elders call this "Temptation." If we take a quick glimpse of this word in particular, we find that dualistically in nature; it presents an excellent breakdown that is relevant to all philosophy in my opinion. Quoted from the tree of knowledge by Alvin Boyd Kuhn. To "Tempt" man would then be to bring his soul down from the realms of spirit, where all religions have asserted that consciousness lies above the human apperception of time." he goes on to state, to "tempt" man would be to subject him to the time consciousness. This type of consciousness comes through the reduction of the higher mind to a lower tempo of vibration as it falls under the limitations of brain activity." We are tempted by the five senses throughout life in our own experiences in this existence with the notion of linear time.

Let's look at the word avatar. I chose that specifically because of the ancient meaning behind it. From Sanskrit means decent from or to cross over. In other words, the decent of the soul and spirit into the matrix, portal, or womb, as the ancient text describes it in our modern-day bible. The cross-over from spiritual substantial reality into mundane temporal reality. What we know as the physical world In Hinduism, this means a manifestation of a deity or released soul into a bodily form. This form is not limited to that of a human. Manifestation can take place on many planes, aspects, and degrees. This definition lets us know that while being born on the earth is something we experience as if it were the start of our existence; it could never be our primal origin because we exist correspondingly on multiple planes and realities. The soul is a deity, a powerful, divine, and eternal aspect of the infinite. According to the ancestors, written in their wonderful legends and folklore, all souls and spiritual manifestations were created in the beginning on the first day according to the 7-day narrative and sent to the material realm at an appointed time, man being a part of this, literally makes the word avatar come to life. "For on the first day, he created the heavens which are above and the earth and the waters and all the spirits which serve before him, the angels of the presence and the angels of sanctification and the angels of the spirit of fire and the angels of the spirit of winds and the angels of the spirit of clouds and of darkness and of snow and of hail and of hoar frost and the angels of the voices and of the thunder and of the lightning and the angels of the spirits of cold and of heat, and of winter and of spring and of autumn and of summer and all of the spirits of his creatures which are in the heavens and in the earth, he created the abysses and the darkness, even tide and night dawn and day which he has prepared in the knowledge of his heart." (See the book of Jubilees)

As we stated previously above, according to another record of the ancestors, from the mind of God, he lowered the highest forms of thought and lifted the lowest forms of thought, and they manifested tangibly. You see, the temple signifies the earthly, which is the lowest plane of creation. I'm sure everyone has heard the bible give the origin of man. Our temples were formed from physical matter or the dust of the earth. "And the Lord god formed {that is created the body of} man from the dust of the ground and breathed into his nostrils the breath of life, and he became a living being {an individual complete in body and spirit.} See the book of Genesis. After researching deeper, we find in some records that man's body can be compartmentalized and classified into and out of different portions of the universe, even the stars and elements. "and on the sixth day, I commanded my wisdom to create man out of the seven components: first, his flesh from the earth; second his blood from dew and from the sun; third; his eyes from the bottomless sea, fourth his bones from stone; fifth his reason from the mobility of angels and from clouds; sixth, his veins and hair from the grass of the earth; seventh his spirit from my spirit and from the wind."See the 2nd book of Enoch.

One major point I would like to make concerning the 5th component of "reason" is that it seems that we as mankind contain within us the power of the mind to think, comprehend, and form judgments and ideals through a process of logic and imagination. These two qualities link to both the objective and subjective mind. It also states our spirit is from Gods very own spirit. According to the Hermeticists, logic Is a masculine aspect, quick, directive, and expressive. Imagination links to the Feminine aspect of the mind. Passive, creative, and generative. Both, when joined harmoniously, are known as "reason" or more famously known as "Hemi-sync," and they seem to be of angelic quality. Specifically, the term used is the "mobility of angels." "Mobility" equates to the swiftness or impulsiveness of our decision-making, while the ancient text itself tells us that humans are gods originally but, through ignorance, will die like men. Researching extensively through multiple accounts in the apocryphal text, we can find ancient wisdom where Jesus explains to the apostles that man is a star and man is also led and governed by stars, referencing the a-parent influence of the astronomical lords. "Lift up your eyes and look to the cloud and the light within it and the stars around it. The star that leads the way is your star; you are a star." See the Gospel of Judas.

It seems the secrets of the papyrus agree, along with modern science, that we are, in fact, multidimensional beings. It is no surprise that scientists have concluded that humans and our galaxy have about 97 percent of the same atoms along with the elements of life. These energies and elements tend to be more prevalent towards the galaxy center, which we mentioned afore time, but to reiterate, according to the writings of Manly

P. Hall, the center of our reality or dimension is essentially the throne of God. Where all life and manifestations yield from. The closer you are to the center, the closer you are to the infinite god. The elements of life are carbon, hydrogen, nitrogen, oxygen, phosphorus, and sulfur. All of which can be found within the micro-universe. This information gives us a cosmic origin that cannot be overlooked. Mentioned in almost every religion are allegories, legends, and myths that include the stars and mankind's involvement with the gods that came from them. What the ancients knew and understood was that each soul is imprinted with cosmic energy as it travels through gates into the vessel it will inhabit for its lifetime on the 3rd-dimensional plane. Being "Born" or "imprinted" with select energy according to the exact time, degree, and angle at which you entered mundane reality. This is not a myth but cosmic law. Yes, the zodiac is a part of our essence, which is a piece of our true self. Think of it this way: your emotional personality is affected by sequences of different energies governed by celestial angles, which affect each of us in a different way. You see, Though the Temple is matter, it is a masterpiece of a creation. The Temple by itself can heal dis-ease, adapt and evolve with its surroundings, conduct energy with or without interference, and is also a receiver of frequencies and vibrations. This amazing body is from the earth, which was created from the darkness of the celestial waters; it is temporal and will go back in accordance with the laws of nature. Dust to Dust and energy to energy. This temple has a counterpart that is married to it until knowledge has been gained and separation from this matrix, meaning the end of a cycle has ensued, which leads us to the second main factor corresponding with the balance of mankind, The Soul.

The soul is eternal and is intrinsic to the stars. This is the second main factor we need to discuss. According to studies of astrology and astronomy, we learn that each house or zodiac in the heavens corresponds differently with the earth and its ruling energies. We can also find use of the zodiac in the ancient writings of the dead seas scrolls and many other religions that predate Jewish folklore. What does that mean for the soul, you ask? Well, for starters, the seven great Lords, which are the ruling luminaries, emit energy directly into our realm, not only affecting people but also, According to Alchemy, which is one of the oldest super occult sciences of any age, the Sun creates Gold, the Moon creates Silver, Mercury creates Mercury, Venus creates Copper, Mars creates Iron, Jupiter creates Tin, and Saturn creates Lead. These precious metals, along with other precious stones such as sapphire, emerald, and clear quartz crystals, have always been the harbinger of man as his senior in creation. Quoted from Gems in style, a well-written blog online, "These metals are the essences of particular Astral Forces, the manifestation of the universal archetypes and their powers that actively interact with our consciousness and affect our well-being in profound ways."

The interesting thing is, as the soul is making its interstellar voyage to this dimension, it starts gathering its attributes and characteristics from each cosmic component before descending to the star gate. For example, imagine life as a video game. You are not the video game, but a piece of your awareness is operating as if it is. In this game, you can choose your avatar and all its qualities and attributes. Theoretically speaking, you have unlimited potential; however, you must grow into your latent abilities through temptation and limitations. As life goes on, you gain wisdom and evolve through the lessons you have learned. Similar to achieving higher levels and upgrades. The really cool thing is not only do we choose the physical characteristics and everything in our surrounding world, but we also choose all of the spiritual elements that make up our piece of consciousness that has chosen to project itself as the "Me" in this reality which is the video game. All of this is done before coming here by angle, energy, and degree; in every aspect, astronomically and numerically, this is the law. As the scripture eloquently states, "in my father's house, there are many mansions." These are the glorious houses prepared for you in the heavens from which you hail. The houses you selected represent what we call the manifestation of you. When the stars align at the exact moment you are ready to be born in the material realm, you carry with you the energy (i.e., characteristics or attributes) stored from different luminaries or planets collectively in your houses to Earth, where you will be able to express that energy the soul was given to have this material experience. Moreover, the objective, according to all of my studies of religion and martial arts, is thus for the soul to transcend the seven lords and the 12 houses and their energetic bonds. Break the archetypal powers and become the sun. The centralized savior of your reality.

The soul is the essence of who we truly are. The soul is the overseer, or the all-seeing eye, patiently watching and learning as your life plays out through your decisions. The manifestation of the collective spiritual living energy in one force. Yes, my friend, the soul is angelic. The soul is not the spirit because the soul, although from God, is divine in itself, on its own accord. Where-as the spirit is divine breath or Ruach in ancient Hebrew, the origin of self-expression. Some great minds and historians link the spirit of God to a magnificent wind vehicle that hovered over the face of the deep as if it were flying, but that's a conversation for another time. If we entertain the theory of the fall of man, we must state one known fact. Mankind has been looking to find the true meaning of life for generations and has not been able to find it. It seems that keen ability was lost with the shift of consciousness throughout the ages. The individual soul must rise and ascend back up in high frequency in order for it to be one with unity. He must raise his reason. Bring his reptilian brain to that of a perfected mind, the consciousness of a god.

As quoted earlier in the ancient text, Jesus says, I and my father are one. How could he think of himself on equal planes as the almighty? This very statement shook the foundation of theoretical doctrine throughout the clergy at that time, but why? It is because the Hebrew sage taught and comprehended the mystic secret that the soul has the capability to do great things far above and beyond Normality. "Verily Verily I say unto you, he that believes on me, the works that I do shall he also do; and greater works than these shall he do; because I go to my father." Man has the tools to realize his magnitude within deep reflection and reciprocate that energy outwardly, therefore changing his environment. The records of the ancestors speak of the realm of souls. This is a place where souls exist prior to coming to the earth. "These things, whatever I have taught you, whatever you have learned, and whatever we have written down, you sit down and write. All the souls of men, whatever of them not yet born and their places, prepared for eternity. For all souls are prepared for eternity before the composition of the earth." (See the writings of Enoch) Its also referenced by Jesus himself saying, "behold, For I will meet you in the realm of souls this day" (See the Aquarian Gospel of Jesus the Christ). At this point, we are one with the father-mother force. We correspond perfectly with the collective, simultaneously as individual minds awaiting our turn to visit this realm. As stated previously above, the soul gains wisdom through trail and temptations. Some wise men call this process the refinery.

Let's look at nature. Each year, it goes through a period of death, but ultimately, it resurrects into life. Thus, the circle of life is in accordance with order. By understanding this cycle, the soul will earn the right to eat from the Tree of Life, which is ultimately Paradise. My soul is my true self; this is the being we must find through internal mediation. We need to be honest about the issues and problems that are brought to us via trials and tribulation. Learning how to cope with deep trauma and completing shadow work, which is the settling of inner turmoil, is necessary for the soul to ascend to a free being. Before we come to this realm, our soul is given a divine spark, which, if the souls didn't have this spark, would not be able to animate the body alone on this material plane. The spark is from the originality and is the most important of the three.

The spirit has been called many names throughout the ancient world. Through shamanistic practices, ritualistic ceremonies, and face-to-face experiences with natural spiritual phenomena, the ancient world gained the notion that the vital spirit is a force that connects every living organism in the cosmos. While connecting all, the spirit simultaneously allows individual expression in different forms of life. I like to think of the spirit as breath or the divine Spark and flame from the originality. This spark connects the soul to the material realm via the vessel by way of breath. This is the heavenly animating force behind all of creation and her creatures. The spirit is the decorator and vital essence that is so powerful and majestic that it transcends dimensions and beings alike. A Divine and Holy Spirit, which is attributed to Wisdom and Feminine Glory. Without the spirit, the body is empty, lifeless, without energy. This happens because the soul, being what we call "created" in the beginning with all the Gods and Goddesses by I AM That I AM (identified by the ancient Hebrews) or awareness, is the pervading energy of infinity.

The spirit or breathe Is the divine feminine aspect of the original I Am being that transcends all dimensions. Both, while distinct and very much different, came from the same source and are eternal, dwelling in a shell within a finite matrix. Without this life force, the expanding of life would not continue. The master soul, who became a light bearer and was called a savior, had this to say concerning breathing. "And Jesus said, Man is the truth and falsehood strangely mixed, for man is breath made flesh; so, truth and falsehood are conjoined in him, and they strive." (See the writings of Levi H. Downing) The breath is like the wind that pulls the leaf off of a withered branch. The breath is similar to a woven basket that carries the infant Moses across still waters. The energy bearer. This is the reason when one learns to control the breath, supernatural power is realized. Here's an interesting gem: did you know Jesus taught that mankind has inborn powers? "And Jesus preached to the Gospel of good will, and peace on earth. He told them of the brotherhood of life, and of the inborn powers of man, and the kingdom of the soul." (See the writings of Levi H. Downing) The immortal soul is in the realm of temporal things. Only when the vessel is clean, and the soul purified will the breath begin to ignite. The spirit will transform the vessel with a heavenly fire as we pass through the third heaven. The rivers of wisdom and knowledge capped with understanding will continue to flow unblocked and balanced with the love of purity. This is not a feat that is easily reached. One must offer his vessel a living sacrifice. This means the practitioner of such a discipline must be aware of his entire being, emotionally, mentally, and consciously. Completely unhinged from the carnality of what we call Life. Living in the aspect of "Now" with his attention on creation. Appreciating every single breath. This is the vital energy coursing through a cosmic being.

CH. 7
THE INBORN POWERS OF MAN

IN ORDER TO BECOME SOMEONE WORTH REMEMBERING, WE MUST FREE OURSELVES FROM THE OPPOSITION, WHICH IS THE PERSON IN THE MIRROR.

To fully utilize human existence, we must tap into that God-given aspect within ourselves. Countless scriptures and papyrus, as well as the legends of old, written on tablets of clay, have all spoken about the angelic essence that was gifted to man. This is not something that is theoretical or fiction, even though its widely presented to us as such. While groundbreaking and influential, the in-depth information concerning these studies is still classified today, with only a few segments being released to the public. Most people are not aware of this information, and regardless of that certitude, this data on supernatural phenomena is actually widely proven amongst the world's most elite military, political, religious, and secret societal structures. Explorations of the mind and willpower of man are not new, for we know that there is nothing new under the centric sun of the universe. The unclassified documents that were released on April 1st, 2008, with a publication date of October 20th, 1973, by none other than the Central Intelligence Agency, identified not only the psychic phenomena within mankind but, in some cases, also its liberation and advocation. Eleanor Criswell, an educator, and psychologist, said in this brief statement, "I want people to know they are normal when they hear voices when they experience visions; we need a psychic liberation, an understanding, and acceptance that psychic experience is not unnatural and is not any illness."

Documented in similar CIA archives are abilities such as astral projection and remote viewing, all of which link to the psychic origin of our eternal substantial essence. In my opinion, the political structures of government are well-versed in these abilities; allegedly, these techniques have been adopted to spy on opposing enemies or even allies during times of war. Allen Cohen, a clinical psychologist, names seven distinct abilities that would be considered a miracle or even dark magic to the non-affirming constituents: "There are seven distinct phenomena; a person usually has one of them, though some rare psychics have combinations of them" He goes on to state the classifications: "Mind reading or the ability to receive telepathic messages. Clairvoyance of the past, future, and present; Vibrational Empathy. The most complex include the ability to heal, read another person's aura, and perceive others' spiritual guides. (I would like to add that almost every one of the above-mentioned psychic gifts has been expressed within all religious legends in some way or form). Psychometry, the ability to know the past of a person or object through touching; and mind force control the most dangerous ability, which includes both the projecting of thoughts into another person's mind as in voodoo and the rare psychokinetic power to bend or alter metals and to make objects dematerialize and rematerialize." Hearing gifts as this starts to open Pandora's box, for each individual is different and has a non-identical relation to how these powers manifest.

To identify these abilities within the ancient religions and legends, we will look at a few sources from ancient Hebrews and some Buddhist customs to support this idea. According to the encyclopedia Brittanica concerning The Buddha and his followers, "There is one, having been one becomes many, appears and vanishes, unhindered he goes through walls, he dives in and out of the earth as if it were water. Without sinking, he walks on water as if on earth. Seated cross-legged, he travels through the sky like a winged bird. With his hand, he touches and strokes the sun and the moon." Coincidentally, the powers of clairvoyance of the past, future, and present reside in a Buddhist technical term called Abhijna, which refers to a set of extraordinary powers and knowledge, including remembrance of past lives, telepathy, clairaudience, clairvoyance, telekinesis, and various other "supernatural" abilities. More importantly, it is the knowledge of the true nature of reality and certainly that one has obtained awakening, which is the highest goal of the Buddhist path. In my opinion, the "awakening" is the goal of all religions ever prostrated in this world. If we want to find evidence of mind reading or the ability to receive telepathic messages, I would like to highlight one of the most famous disciples, Simon Peter, and the story of the death of Ananias and his wife. Simon Peter was able to perceive the unjust business deal given to him by using the Spirit or divine intuition. He gave credit to knowing the intent of the swindlers by means of spirituality or, in other words, psychic phenomena. Both offenders dropped dead in the aftermath. There are many more instances like this throughout the Bible.

Delores Cannon, documented in her book Jesus and the Essenes, is a story similar to the Tower of Babel. I brought this incident into the conversation because here, between the text, we find a theory pertaining to supernatural abilities. "If we do this great thing, we can become as great as Yahweh and find a way to be even greater and have more power. And because of this, it had been lost, and confusion was brought. Yahweh took away this ability, and man was struck dumb because he had never had to communicate with others in any other way. And it was a great loss. Then he learned to speak with his mouth with words; before this, there was no need." This signifies the idea that man lost the ability to use his telepathic powers and had to communicate primitively through words. (See the writings of Delores Cannon) The ability to heal is considered one of the most complex psychic gifts, and yet, according to the philosophers, everyone has the capability to tap into that energy. It seems it's a point of believing more than it is a mystical experience. One of the most famous healers of the Piscean age was none other than Jesus and, in this particular legend, according to the Aquarian gospel, a master teaching him the art of healing states, "Of course the will of man is remedy supreme and by the vigorous exercise of will, man will make tense a chord that is relaxed, or may relax one that is too tense, and thus may heal himself." Here again, going back to "believing" and controlling the mind to ultimately use the power of "healing."

In today's world, there are great masterminds of healing who have the power to change the course of the health industry right now! With just the act of them touching and correcting the energy flow in the body or the use of the higher faculty of mind, namely "will," to impress the process of healing, in turn making the patient "believe" he is healed and thus, the patient is healed. A lot of the healing sciences are considered "conspiracy," yet all truths are but half-truths in the dynamic of reality. Think intently on your palms and the soles of your feet. You can feel the sensation of the energy coursing through your entire being. According to the writings of Manly P. Hall concerning the allegory of the Crucifixion of Christ, "The passion nails are highly important symbols when it is realized that according to the esoteric systems of culture, there are certain secret centers of force in the Palms of the hands and in the soles of the feet." It is here where the idea of energy transfer, healing, physical, and energetic manipulation through elements from breath drawn in the body manifests itself. Covered previously, we know that the body can absorb and exude energy, especially if we reside in an area that complements our element. The environment around us can heal or hinder our bodies. Similar to my favorite anime, DragonBall, the human vessel has what scientists and physicists call an "aura" around it that emanates a certain color, depending on your emotional frequency.

This aura can be manipulated and controlled for flight, telekinesis, healing, and many other superhuman abilities. Some of these abilities may seem so extreme that they would break the concept of reality, causing the individual who has reached this plateau to be mistaken as a magician or sorcerer. Interestingly, I have aspirations of utilizing my aura for combat, flight, instant relocation, and galaxy travel. All of these are things you see in anime shows all across the world. What sparks my interest is the fact that energy control, aura manipulation, and cymatic frequencies are joined together, bringing ultimate realization to the art of the practitioner. When you learn to control that essence within your own body, raising that sensation with every breath or lowering that sensation to a lesser point of the body, there will be the power of supermen or superwomen. There is one legend that I would like to highlight from the book of Jasher, which is another ancient Hebrew writing. Judah, son of Israel, utilized his aura control and cymatic frequencies similar to Goku from dragon ball, causing much damage to Egypt. In other words, he was powering up his vessel and made a mess. "And Judah hastened and drew his sword and uttered a loud, bitter scream, and he smote with his sword, and he sprang upon the ground, and he still continued to shout against all the people. And when he did this thing, the lord caused the terror of Judah and his brethren to fall upon the valiant men and all the people that surrounded them. And they all fled at the sound of the shouting, and they were terrified and fell one upon the other, and many of them died as they fell, and they all fled from before Judah and his brethren and before Joseph. And whist they were fleeing, Judah and his brethren pursued them unto the house of the pharaoh, and they all escaped, and Judah again sat before Joseph and roared at him like a lion and gave a great tremendous shriek at him. And the shriek was heard at a distance, and all inhabitants of Succoth heard it, and all Egypt quaked at the sound of the shriek, and also the walls of Egypt and of the land of Goshen fell in from the shaking of the earth, and pharaoh also fell from his throne upon the ground, and also all the pregnant women of Egypt and Goshen miscarried when they heard the noise of the shaking, for they were terribly afraid."

Historians site the land of Sukkoth and Goshen anywhere from 75 miles to 120 miles from the land of Egypt. Can you picture hearing a war shriek so loud that it's heard from over 100 miles away? The power of this shriek caused multiple deaths and an earthquake! Seems supernatural to me. The innate power within us seems to be able to conjure up some devastating power! Moreover, for the ability to see spirit guides, I would like to point out the epic tale of kings and conquerors in the Old Testament of the Hebrews, "And he answered, fear not for they that be with us are more than they that be with them. And Elisha prayed and said, lord, I pray thee, open his eyes that he may see, and the lord opened the eyes of the young man; and he saw: and behold the mountain was full of horses and chariots of fire round about Elisha." This is a perfect example of a psychic experience where the young boy was able to see the spirits or angels guiding the prophet. These spirit guides or angels are always around every being in this universe. Nothing escapes the EYE OF THE ALL.

Regarding the ability to read the aura of a human being, I would like to site the Old Testament patriarch Moses and his legend conversing with the being Yahweh aka AHAYAH (I AM), referred to by the ancient Hebrews, but better known as Lord Enlil of the Eden, the Sumerian deity of old. "And it came to past when Moses came down from mount Sinai with the two tables of testimony in Moses' hand, when he came down from the mount, that Moses wist not that the skin of his face shone while he talked with him. And when Arron and all the children of Israel saw Moses, behold, the skin of his face shone; and they were afraid to come nigh." Another text recording this exact incident states, "He came from the mountains with the laws of God, and it is said that he was shining, that even the air about him shimmered" (see Jesus and the Essenes). If we use a little thought, we can see that at this point, either Moses was in so much power and energy that it seems his vessel absorbed some fragments of the deity, or the vibration of Moses was so immensely high on the scale of frequency after this encounter that other humans could easily perceive the godly halo or aura emanating from off of the Patriarch. Finally, the domaine of the gods, along with their vast technology, can change the physical, spiritual, and energetic composition of man. Which previously discussed allegedly happened already in the ancient past.

In her writings, the wonderful psychic and mystic Delores Cannon spoke about the ancient Essenes' perception of auras while healing. "It looked like a glow of light from, say, his hand to the affected part of the person's body, and their auras would start to glow brighter to where people who ordinarily did not see the aura could see their auras." (See Jesus and the Essenes) Another instance of humans sensing an aura is written on Enki's tablets. "My life sense returned to me, as if I was in some kind of an enclosure. It was dark, but there was also an aura, and then my name was called again by the deepest of voices. And although I could hear it, I could not tell where the voice came nor could I see whoever it was that spoke, and I said here I am." Whichever way we lean-to, we can begin to see this mystery unfold. In psychometry, we have modern-day specialists who focus on this phenomenon, and I am sure it wouldn't take an extensive amount of time to find this documented. Mind force control is the most dangerous ability, which includes both the projecting of thoughts into another persons mind as in voodoo and the rare psychokinetic power to bend or alter metals and to make objects dematerialize and rematerialize; things like this are discussed in the writings of the ancient Egyptians and the Emerald tablets of Thoth the Atlantean. Oddly enough, this sounds exactly like something out of a Stan Lee or Stephen King film.

I would be amiss if I didn't mention the correspondence between the classified fictional superheroes and the psychic phenomena inside the average man. Clearly, these abilities portrayed on the big screen have originated from inside the most powerful conductors of DNA in the human body, that is, the heart, the brain, and the gut. Genetic information. Once these faculties are intertwined, they produce a frequency called gnosis, which is elaborated in the ancient text from the gnostic view. Nonetheless, that is only a school of thought. The secret of this ancient concept is that when you know yourself at that particular level, you will also come to know God because you will discover that the divine is within you. After studying the synchronizations of the legends of the ages, we can find most of these exact powers and abilities within its ancient archives and grounded in its ancient myths. We must also remember there is so much we have yet to discover and uncover in the world of mystery. These techniques are no longer "theory," as psychologists and scientists alike are baffled after numerous experiments and exercises that seem to prove that fiction is more reality than we have been led to believe. Yes, these psychic powers have been chronicled in literature for decades, and even far beyond that extent (if we begin to speak in terms of religious doctrine), they are found within the legends of every nation on this earth today. In my own studies, I've found that intuition is another psychic ability because, through this higher mental faculty, a person can psychically maneuver in such a way that appears to be mysterious and spiritually inclined. All the while, his mind is constantly interchanging and receiving information back and forth from the higher planes of thought to the lower planes of thought, all mentally and psychically.

There are excellent legends compiled from the culture of the Hebrews, and many of the supernatural powers spoken of have been documented through religious history, such as superhuman strength and superhuman speed. Immediately, I think of Superman or the flash. I'm sure we are all familiar with these two fictional characters and their heroisms on the big screen. These things are not limited to that; in our modern world, men and women show amazing acts of abilities we can only think of. For example, in the Shaolin Monastery of olden times, these masters of energy utilized meditation as a way to project the energy from within themselves outwardly. Physically defying the odds of what is naturally bearable for the average human body. The key to understanding this is to have the knowledge of what's within, as well as the knowledge and control of breath. These practitioners of the natural law were average men who, with reason and contemplation, understood that there was something operating around them that was greater than just being human. They found that this something can be harnessed. For superhuman strength and speed, let's take a look at the ancient book of the Twelve Patriarchs, where we see these powers in action. "And the lord showed me favor in all my ways both in the field and in the house. I know that I raced a hind and caught it and prepared the meat for my father, and he did eat. And the roes I used to master in the chase and overtake all that was in the plains. A wild mare I overtook and caught and tamed it. I slew a lion and plucked a kid out of its mouth. I took a bear by its paw and hurled it down the cliff, and it was crushed. I outran the wild boar and seized it. As I ran, I threw it in sunder. A leopard in Hebron leaped upon my dog, and I caught it by the tail and hurled it on the rocks. It was broken in twain. I found a wild ox feeding in the fields and seizing it by the horns and whirling it round and stunning it, cast it from me and slew it."

When researching the animals depicted in this legend, it becomes apparent these aren't your average ordinary men. A hind is a modern-day deer, and it can run anywhere from 37 mph to 50 mph; a Roe is compared to a gazelle, which can run anywhere from 30 mph to 60 mph. A wild mare is said to have a length of about 8ft long and weigh 660 pounds, and here Judah, the son of Jacob and patriarch of the tribe of kings, is said to have overtaken them. The bite force of a lion is about 650 psi, and they can easily weigh anywhere from 250 lbs to 450 lbs. Judah is said to have slain this lion and taken a kid out of its mouth. A bear can be anywhere from 250 lbs to 500 lbs and can stand anywhere from 5-6 feet. Judah is said to have grabbed it by its paw and thrown it off a cliff until it was crushed. A wild bore can be anywhere from 170-180 lbs and run from 20- 30mph. Judah tore it apart while running! A leopard can weigh about 70 pounds, but how hard do you think Judah would have to swing the animal to break it in two? A wild ox is roughly about 1500 lbs to 3000 lbs. Judah is said to have whirled it around by the horns and thrown it, ultimately killing it. I decided to quantify this piece by piece so you can see the magnificence and splendor of superhuman abilities written in the legends.

Let's find another example. "A man of Giant stature I found hurling Javlins before and behind as he sat on horseback. And I took up a stone of sixty pounds weight and hurled it and smote his horse and killed it." Even in modern-day extreme strength sports, you cannot find a human strong enough to throw a sixty-pound rock and kill anything, let alone a war horse. Here is another son of Israel showing his example of super strength. "I was valiant in keeping the flocks. Accordingly, I guarded at night the flock, and whenever the lion came or the wolf, or any wild beast against the fold, I pursued It, and overtaking it, I seized its foot with my hand and hurled it about a stone's throw, and so killed it." Now let's think about "a stone's throw" this would implicate that as far as a man could throw a stone that could fit within his hand, that is how far away these beasts were being thrown to their death. A stones throw is a short distance, but to throw an animal, that's an insane feat! If that isn't superhuman strength, then I don't know what is. Another son of Jacob Naphtali was a man with superhuman speed. He was so fast and light-footed that he could run on the ears of corn and not break them. This reminds me of the action film Crouching Tiger Hidden Dragon, where we see this in action many times as the martial artists soar across the TV screen, practically tiptoeing like a ballerina. "And Judah spoke to his brother Naphtali, and he said unto him, make haste go now and number all of the streets of Egypt and come and tell me, and Simeon said unto him, let not this thing be trouble to thee; now I will go to the mount and take up one large stone for the mount and level it at everyone in Egypt, and kill all that were in it. And Naphtali went as Judah had commanded him, for Naphtali was light-footed as one of the swift stags, and he would go upon the ears of corn, and they would not break under him."

As I have been showing everyone this day, it seems that the ancient text has marvelous stories and feats of supernatural abilities on both psychic and supernatural phenomena. Judah, the king of the twelve tribes, is particularly highlighted due to him being the leader of all the nation of Israel at that time. My question to the readers of this treatise is this: could you do these things? "And when Judah heard this thing, he was exceedingly wroth, and his anger burned within him, and there was before him in that place a stone, the weight of which was about 400 shekels, (about 10 pounds) and Judah's anger was kindled, and he took the stone in one hand and cast it to the heavens and caught it with his left hand. And he placed it afterward under his legs, and he sat upon it with all his strength, and the stone was turned into dust from the force of Judah." From my comprehension, there aren't too many men in history who could do such a thing. As students of research, we can begin to find many more correlations between activities like this in the scriptures but let us go to one last example of an amazing war story. "And the sons of Jacob girt on their weapons of war, and they took in their hands each man his shield and his javelin, and they approached the battle. Judah, the son of Jacob ran first before his brethren and ten of his servants, and he went towards these kings. And Jashub king of Tapnach also came forth with his army before Judah, and Judah saw Jashub and his army coming toward him, and Judah wrath was kindled, and his anger burned before him, and he approached the battle in which Judah ventured his life. Jashub and his entire army were advancing towards Judah, and he was riding a very strong and powerful horse. Jashub was a valiant man covered with iron and brass from head to foot. And whilst he was upon the horse, he shot arrows with both hands from before and behind, as was his manner in all his battles, and he never misses the place to where he aimed his arrows. When Jashub came to fight against Judah and darted many arrows against Judah, the lord bound Jashub's hand, and the arrows that he shot rebounded against his own men. And notwithstanding this, Jashub kept advancing towards Judah to challenge him with the arrows, but the stance between them was about 30 cubits, and when Judah saw Jashub darting forth his arrows against him, he ran to him with his wrath-excited might.

And Judah took up a long stone from the ground, and its weight was sixty shekels, and Judah ran towards Jashub, and with the stone struck him on the shield, and Jashub was stunned with the blow and fell off from his horse to the ground. The shield burst asunder out of the hand of Jashub and, through the force of the blow, sprang to the distance of about 15 cubits, and the shield fell before the second camp. The kings that were with Jashub saw from a distance the strength of Judah, the son of Jacob, and what he had done to Jashub, and they were terribly afraid of Judah. And They assembled near Jashub camp seeing his confusion, and Judah drew his sword and smote 42 men of the camp of Jashub, and the whole of Jashub camp fled before

Judah, and no man stood against him, and they left Jashub and fled from him, and Jashub was prostrate on the ground." In the biblical text, the God of Israel would intervene in the wars of men in miraculous sorts, and as we can see, the power of these men was unmatched. Judah, by himself, was able to take out over 42 warriors with the powers bestowed upon him! At the climax of the battle, over 15000 men were destroyed by the sons of Israel. There are many legends of the men of renown, the Demi-gods of old, and their war explorations. For example, in the Greek legends, Achilles was a man-God who had the power to slay half of an army by himself, and the other half would flee before his face. So, one man slaying 42 men to me is a minor feat to these famed warriors.

You may ask, is there only one way to master the inner energy? According to my research, the answer is no. There are many ways, but only one way to maintain energy. This way is displayed in the lives of the ascended masters depending on what culture you may have emerged from. This is the life. One of balance, harmony, and peace. When you look at the earth, some say that she has a spirit. "Mother Earth," some say that she lives and breathes. Is there not a spiritual counterpart to the physical? Do you agree that we, being the soul, came from the cosmos, but our bodies, which are the vehicles used to experience this realm, came from the earth, which is ultimately still a part of the cosmos? Once this is understood, we can perceive that there is a spirit behind all living things, and to embody this spirit, we must be in balance with nature. Once we begin to get in tune with the vibrational frequency of God, we begin to realize many things concerning the internal power of men. One concept I like to relay corresponds with what we read in ancient texts. "I can do all things through Christ which strengthens me." (See the Epistle to the Philippians) This "Christ" is an external version of the higher self. Its god given and can be joined together with the soul because it is a part of you.

These things sound very mystical; however, they are as simple as nature. Humans have had abilities since the very beginning. All of ancient cultures and societies refer to a fall of man or a fall of consciousness. It seems we have lost our true nature for a shadow of mortality, but the masters of mind who have all come here have expressed from within themselves power and miracles. This shows us that we could do the same if we had the discipline and oneness to realize it. There are many examples of the coherent power of man. The CIA and many other government agencies have begun to figure out the mysteries of the mind. Natural healing doctors, such as reiki practitioners around the world, have practiced the use of energy transfer to heal energetically. Masters of mind and thought have used Meditation to heal on a mental level, joined with the use of hand "Mudras" which is another form of healing that multiplies the effects of meditation. The only stumbling block in front of man is his own mentality and his own belief systems. If a man doesn't have his own mind in check, then he cannot express himself outside of the bounds of space and time. It is said that our reality is controlled by how we think. Why? Well, we covered the electric idea earlier in this work. Our thoughts send electric signals to the universe; these signals then run a loop, so to speak. This means that the universe sends the same energy back to us, identically matching what we put out and what we have been thinking, which also means that our thoughts create our entire reality. So, it is very important to assess every situation positively because man unknowingly is the master of his entire existence. Once this is realized, we can grab hold of life and simply create. All while spreading the gospel of goodwill towards men and peace on earth.

CH.8
THE BATTLE OF THE GODS

TO BE ONE WITH ANY FORCE, THE CATALYST MUST MATCH FORCE IN FREQUENCY

When speaking about this philosophy, many have asked how I can reference the Bible or the writings of ancient societies and cultures to support martial arts. What are the correspondences between religion and fighting techniques of war? Well, my response to that amazing question will be answered in the following paragraphs of this chapter, which may be one of the most important sections of this book. In my opinion, Martial Arts has soul truths that will bring self-realization, and ultimately, that is true spirituality. The ancient Patriarchs of old were the sages and masters of minds from some of the most powerful nations of the world. These nations were given the rule of law and innovation by none other than the so-called fallen gods themselves. Gifted the power to kick-start civilizations and pass on secret teachings to the initiated and informed, the hierophants of these nations were truly descendants of the gods. An excerpt from the translated tablets says, "While fates we decreed, the hand of destiny every step directed! Did Anu say, the will of the creator of all is clear to see: On earth and for Earthlings, only emissaries we are. The earth to the Earthlings belongs, to preserve and advance them we were intended! If that is our mission here, let us act accordingly! So did Enki say. The great Anunnaki, who the fates decree counsels exchanged regarding the land: To create civilized regions the great Anunnaki decided, therein knowledge to mankind provide; Cities of man to establish, therein in sacred precincts abodes for the Anunnaki create; Kingship as on Nibiru on Earth establish, Crown and scepter to a chosen man give; by him the word of the Anunnaki to the people convey, work and dexterity to enforce; In the sacred precincts a priesthood to establish, the Anunnaki as lofty lords to serve and worship. Secret knowledge to be taught, civilization to humankind convey." (See The Lost Book of Enki)

As covered earlier in a previous section, we spoke about the lesser knowledge given to man. This information was passed on to mankind with a directive that would give way to much turmoil in the world of men. One piece of this knowledge happened to be the art of warfare to conquer and control peoples, nations, and tongues. There are many legends of the Israelite warriors doing wondrous battle moves and techniques in the midst of war, which we have covered. Most of these battles were removed from the confines of our modern-day bible only to be revealed in the secret apocryphal text, which has been highly discredited by some mainstream religious leaders. Nonetheless, they provide an excellent source of information and insight. The battles of the Greek gods and goddesses, the conflicts of the Demi-gods of ancient Uruk, and the clash between the olden gods of Egypt all have a synchronized place in this origin of knowledge given to man. The mystery of this knowledge is only a minuscule component of a much grander genesis. You see the legends of the ancestors, who tell tales of many glorified battles of the ancient pantheons throughout the ages. The men of valor, sages and magicians, warlords, and tyrants alike fought in honor or condemnation, peace and chaos. Blood and bone of the righteous and unrighteous were offered upon the battlefield of the gods, leaving only the strongest and most skilled entities standing. Even though many would fall in their conquests, their stories were eternally engraved in the codex of all ancient religions and philosophies through allegories and historical wonders of the world. Going back to some of the earliest texts concerning these battles, we find that this lesser knowledge was, in fact, an ancient secret disclosed to man, but even these secrets have levels within them that would bring about the emergence of something greater. In my opinion, namely enlightenment. I have already proven to you that there have been celestial battles throughout our entire history; it seems the movie Star Wars is nothing short of a soft illustration of our ancient past.

According to our ancestors, the Gods of all ancient religions and customs, under the presence of the holy breath, created all so-called earthly and spiritual beings. These created beings have an internal psychic operation, and all of its executions originate in what we call God and from God. According to the ancient Hebrew text, warfare seems second nature to the god of Israel. Not only that god but also every other major higher being in the ancient text had a background in warfare. According to the biblical narrative, we see both good and evil being created in balance, as well as both of its components. "I form light and create darkness: I make peace and create evil: I the lord do all these things." (See the writings of the prophet Isaiah) So, the essence of war and combat derives from the god of Israel himself, along with the seven great spirits that govern this realm. That would mean it also originates from the creative light. Let's allow that to sink in momentarily. Some may be shocked to understand that something as carnal as war could originate from a place of absolute peace or from a god of absolute benevolence. Surely you have heard the phrase "order out of chaos" correct? Well, you can find that phrase on the back of our American dollar and around the pyramid. Simply put, in order for a stagnant existence to morph or evolve into its true purpose, there must be a shifting force, and this force is a factor that causes a breakthrough. Thereby changing the course of dominating thoughts. Therefore, peace and chaos must always be intertwined in the realm of men. There is a well-known quote made extremely famous in recent times by an excellent mind, soul, and scientist, Neil DeGrasse, "if there is a God, God is either not all-powerful or not all good." In my opinion, if we start to ponder the essence of good and evil and the degree of polarity between them both, we will find that all truths are but half-truths, and good and evil from an energetic perspective are the same thing. According to biblical legend, a war broke out in the first realm. Which is not on the physical plane we are currently experiencing. A tumult between the Gods and Goddesses of heaven, down to the holy mountains of the gods. Synchronized through Mount Hermon in Hebraic culture and Mount Olympus in Greek culture. Hence, "The Battle of The Gods"

The Bible teaches us that a Great War broke out in heaven before our realm was created. What a beautiful prophetic writing. "And there was war in heaven Michael and his angels fought against the dragon and the dragon fought and his angels and prevailed not; neither was their place found any more in heaven. And the great dragon was cast out, that old serpent, called the devil, and satan which deceiveth the whole world: he was cast out to the earth, and his angels were cast out with him." This is one of the most mystical and disputed books within the King James Bible. Not only was this book, at one point in time, arguably not credited to be profitable scripture, but according to those who deem its contents worthy, it seems to be one of the biggest portions of prophecy concerning world events today. Michael, the archangel, being one of the most powerful angels in heaven, essentially coined the champion and warrior of the nation of Israel. It is he who intercedes on their behalf, leading the charge against Satan, the deceiver and God of destruction. Now, when looking at this, we must ask ourselves this question. What is war to a god? What is war to the angelic forces of the heavens? Here, we reference the hermetic axiom, as above so below. We can understand what heavenly or cosmic war is by seeing how we carry it out today. Even with technology such as AI, we can illustrate an astounding angelic war, which can give us a glimpse of these mystical forces. The militant organizations of the world study extensively different forms of martial arts, energy, and element manipulation, so by universal law, we can assume the gods or angels do so as well. Only on a grander scale in terms of power and capability.

Technology is also utilized within combat, but the technology of the gods far exceeds anything that we have today. Great minds of the modern day estimate the technology of those who orchestrate the government far exceeds anything the public is aware of by centuries. Interestingly enough, the ancient tablets describe the technology used to raise the dead, procure long-life, rejuvenation of the body, and much more. These stories were inscribed in clay thousands of years ago. We can only imagine the types of weapons that were being used in this ancient celestial battle. In fact, written in the tablets, the Anunnaki pilot Anzu was sentenced to death and vaporized with ray gun technology for sins and crimes against the crown. "Death by execution, the seven judged Anzu. With a Killing Ray, Anzu's life breath was extinguished. Let his body to the vultures be left Ninurta said," In 2019, the U.S. Air Force developed the world's first combat-ready high energy laser, capable of scaling up to 50kw. That's enough to destroy attacking drones and mortar rounds. Oh yes, this is actual tech, and the Anunnaki had weapons that were 100 times more catastrophic and technology that was much more advanced. You see, along with the technology from other worlds came every fighting style in terms of martial arts. Each fighting force of elements and psychic phenomena originated from the spirit that is placed within man depending on genetics and the unique capabilities of the avatar.

The use of fire, water, earth, air, lightning, wind, ice, thunder, etc., appear as elements and forces on the earth but are spiritual in their core foundation. All of these are used to govern natural life, but all these also can be used to take life in the grand circle of nature. I would like to compare this battle between Michael and the angels to the tournament of power in the anime Dragon Ball Super. This excellent anime gives an esoteric insight to the public, with its audience believing that it is just a show and nothing more. In this anime, you see many different gods and angels. Each has its own selected power and force to control. They each have their own fighting style and champions in control of their realm. Numbered by order, power, and rank in terms of supremacy and succession. Similar to what we have been discussing here and what we will be discussing later. With enough research, you will find that the gods of old are a part of a royal hierarchy with order and rank, as well as a scepter and crown. These beings operated under universal law, using the secrets of otherworldly travel under the all. A measure of these secrets was taught to men from the line of the biblical Shem. If you think about it like this, the pages of revelation start to come alive, especially when we correspond this legend with the historical fables all throughout history.

This battle between the heavenly forces and angels of darkness can also correspond with the Babylonian myth of Ethana and Zu, who were led by pride to strive for the highest seat among the star gods on the northern mountain of the gods. Sounds similar to the writings of the prophet Isaiah when he describes Lucifer, the light bringer falling from heaven, and the lofty spells and decrees the archetype deliberated. We also can find some correspondence in the Dead Sea scrolls, namely the war scrolls, according to Menahem Mansoor, the angels of light who are identified with Michael, the prince of light, fighting against the angels of darkness. These scrolls are ancient and highly recognized as some of the oldest accounts of the Hebraic version of history. Once again, this gives us a profound insight into the battle between these celestial beings in the realm of the gods.

Written in the archives of history, Within Greek Mythology, ancient Babylonian mythology, ancient Sumerian mythology, etc., we can find all the stories and legends pertaining to this great battle specified in the King James Bible and many others. It just so happens that the stories are relayed differently to its people. There are also many other great and terrible battles that captivated mankind throughout time, detailing when the Gods and goddesses fought for supremacy. I'm sure you have heard of the Clash of the Titans. The legends of the offspring of these Gods ruled the earth and would devour men while causing wars and famine to spread across the land. Well, this battle concerning the First World and the fathers of all of these different ideals and ancient stories was so detrimental that it produced a chain reaction that would change the entire course of the realm. As I stated earlier, each spiritual being in the First World had its own order; they had their own particular source of power they were in control of. This means that each God or higher intellectual being has its own course or movements. Similar to the course of the stars, which are considered living, moving beings of light by many schools of thought today. I have corresponded my last assertion with the words of Marduk written in the ancient tablets. I believe this will give you an idea of the gods being excellent in their own faction and discipline. "So did Marduk as Ra above all other gods himself emplace. Their powers and attributes to himself, he by himself assigned: As Enlil, I am for lordship and decrees, as Ninurta for the hoe and Combat; As Adad for lightning and thunder, As Nanar for illuminating the night; As Utu I am Shamas, (the all-seeing Mesopotamian god of the sun) As Nergal over the lower worlds I reign; As Gibil the golden depths I know, whence copper and silver come I have found; As Ningishzidda numbers and their count I command, the heavens my glory bespeak. By these proclamations, the Anunnaki leaders were greatly alarmed."

As you can see, the gods take their rank and role very seriously, and in my opinion, our destiny has all been tied together, with our present future ever-knowing and changing. As stated above, in a previous chapter, we referenced the records of the Hebrews in the book of Jubilees and how when God created all the spirits on the first day, he gave them a particular set of skills. As we covered earlier, these skills are attributes and natural orders. The Elemental beings in charge have complete autonomy controlling it and how it manifests on this earth. Correspondingly, in terms of the four elements and nature spirits, the great Paracelsus believed the following statement written from the secret teachings of all ages: "Paracelus believed that each of the four primary elements known to the ancients as earth, fire, air, and water consisted of a subtle, vaporous principle and a gross corporeal substance." This means they have higher faculties, which we aren't aware of, and lower faculties, which directly affect us. He goes on to state,

"Being without man's compound organism and lacking his spiritual and intellectual vehicles, the nature spirits are subhuman in their rational intelligence, but from their functions-limited to one element- has resulted in a specialized type of intelligence far ahead of man in those lines of research peculiar to the element in which they exist." (See the secret teachings of all ages) This means, ladies and gentlemen, that no matter what we have learned in this physical realm regarding the four elements, a higher level of knowledge is hidden behind the gross physical veil. By this, we know that all the elements will not manifest on this plane if there isn't a spirit attached to it that generates that particular force in accordance with natural law. Collectively, These pervading spiritual beings have the power to control the elements and all manner of force or psychic phenomena. What comes to your mind when you think of this? Sounds like a page right out of X-men, right, or maybe Marvel? Well, I am grateful to entertain such a fantasy. Let's open our minds to the concept of each spirit having its own order and its own particular set of skills. These spirits, although naturally endowed with the essence of the Creator, can make war and carry out vengeance upon whomever. This could explain some of the natural disasters we see around the earth. Or maybe, on a lower level, it just simply gives us insight into how the unseen manipulates and governs our entire reality.

Let me use an example from one of my favorite shows in anime, called "Avatar: the last air bender." If you aren't familiar with this show or do not quite remember, let's enlighten you. This show was based upon a monk who possessed the power of the element air, but not only that. He also had the ability to control all the elements and bring balance to the world, including Water, Earth, Fire, and Ether. According to some philosophies, every human contains within the body all five elements. "It is widely believed that the human structure is a miniature form of the universe that is made up of five elements- Fire, air, water, earth, and sky. These elements are present in fixed proportions, and even the slightest imbalance of any of these can be disastrous." It is said that the human hand is directly correlated with these types of energies within the body. "Hands have a power of their own; through the regular practice of various Mudras, a person could control his life." This statement was quoted from Acharya Keshav, a well-known mystic and yoga practitioner. We now can begin to understand the power of energy and how we set about to manipulate that force. "There is a tremendous flow of energy in our hands, and each finger represents one of the five elements- the thumb Agni (fire), the forefinger is vayu (air), the middle finger is Akash (ether), the ring finger is Prithvi (earth) and the little finger is jal (water)." There is no denying that mankind contains nature, as nature is mankind itself.

This character, whose name was Aang, was the last individual who could manipulate all elements naturally. His goal was to master the four lower elements while mastering the 5th element, which is called ether, spirit, or sky, and save the world from its destruction. The 5th element is the ability to access the books of life, paradise, or the Akashic records. You may ask how the 5th element is linked to these states of consciousness. Well, these states of consciousness are energetically embedded in the DNA of humans and connected to the knowledge of the cosmos.

Once again, we must remember that we are but a miniature universe to a much bigger universe. The characters in this anime call this frequency the "avatar state," where Aang could access the information of his countless past lives and utilize the knowledge and power as such. According to the ancestors of old, this is paradise, the third heaven, the Halls of Amenti or Zen consciousness. Where the rejuvenation of energy occurs. As I mentioned before, according to esoteric teachings, this awakened consciousness manifests when the holy anointing oil of God descends and anoints the individual. Making him a son of God or a Christ. An obvious allegory for the natural bodily functions such as the rising of the kundalini and the descent of the Christ seed to the base of the solar plexus. This is why the apostle Philip states in the Gnostics that one no longer is a follower of Christ but has now become a Christ. "But one receives them in the anointing of the power of the cross; the apostles call it the right and the left. For this reason, one is no longer a Christian but a Christ" (see the Gospel of Phillip). "The right and left" corresponds to the right and left hemispheres of the brain and what happens when a man or woman bring in harmony these two polarized energies. Scientists call this "Hemi-sync". The scriptures once again eloquently mask the alchemical process of illumination from base man to God or air bender to avatar state.

The anime cartoons we watch correspond with religion in many ways. Interestingly, according to the Aquarian gospel of Jesus the Christ, when the world is in need of greater light, a beacon, so to speak, in a world of darkness, or in need of a bright star to a world that cannot see, a master soul is sent to lead the

111

way and guide mankind into higher states of consciousness. "And so, the holy ones have judged; when men have needed added light, a master soul has come to the earth to give the light. Before the Vedic days, the world had many sacred books to light the way; and when men needed greater light, the Vedas, the Avesta, and the books of Tao appeared to show the way to greater heights" (see The Aquarian gospel of Jesus the Christ" There can be many Christs as stated in the Bible, just as there are many antichrists, but allegedly only one master soul in these ages to set the standard. I.e., the Buddha, after him, the one they call Jesus. Similarly, there is only one avatar that can change the course of the world during a lifetime. It is said only those who have mastered self while laying to rest the carnal man and his desires can enter paradise. Hence, "the lord is my Shepard I shall not want." (see the writings of King David) Similar to Jacob wrestling with the angel of God. Only to prevail and be renamed Israel, for you have power with God. We have mentioned the esoteric meaning behind the name of Israel in this writing.

What is interesting about the four elements is that in Greek philosophy, these natural forces could be likened to states of consciousness. Each state of consciousness unlocks more knowledge and abilities that ultimately enhance the human anatomy and experience. Discussed and deliberated by great minds such as Hippocrates and Aristotle, these thought concepts are mind-boggling to this day. In this anime, Avatar the Last Air Bender, each element had a particular set of movements needed in order to physically manipulate its energy efficiently and masterfully. These elements were directly correlated to a different nation, creed, or culture with its own individual fighting style. It is said in correspondence with the philosophers that to be one with any force; the catalyst must match force in frequency. In other words, any tool or power one wields must become an extension of you, therefore becoming one source. Energetically or physically. In this case, the gods of the old used martial arts, energy manipulation, telekinesis, and other psychic, elemental, and metaphysical attributes. These martial arts forms would connect the body, soul, and spirit with the element that is engraved in the practitioner's DNA. As we covered before, DNA is the source that connects us to the unlimited god within and without. The DNA of the practitioner is only the temporary aspect of this virtue because prior to this physical experience, our cosmic fingerprint was generated in the stars and fulfilled in the cosmos.

If you ask me, it seems fitting to say that the gods from the beginning and all the ancient spirits created knew how to make war and create peace, for they are but extensions of the one source. They knew how to control and manipulate the element they were assigned by the creator, or any other element at that. Whether it be with alien technology or scientific methods beyond our wildest dreams, the case is remarkably interesting. You see the hidden power of the human mind, where the soul sits, lies the ability to create worlds or destroy them. Create utopias or begat anguish, the god within and without, only if man could perceive his true origin. Locked in the confines of this area is untapped potential and power. When we study nature, we can see how each creature not only corresponds correctly with its environment but also understands its place with an almost God-given intuition. Does not nature show forth her beauty in a cyclic fashion? Humanity, being God's most precious creation and the highest level of expression in this realm, also follows this suit. The ancient sages knew that the internal is where power is owned, which is the essence of the creator's breath and light. Within this secret knowledge, the wise gain strength and wisdom. So, when I make an assertion and say, "Martial arts began in the heavens," I am not referring to one set of martial arts. By default, all fighting styles and warfare have their primal origin in the first world. In the realm of light, which is spiritual. How you say? Well, because the first war was spiritual, between spiritual beings who could manipulate the elements as well as the clouds, thunder, and lightning. They also had knowledge of every type of warfare and weaponry known to man and even knowledge that is unknown. As we continue to push the veil, everything that we have been conditioned to believe will be challenged for those who seek it.

According to legend, out of peace came chaos, and the leader of that chaos, called the dragon, was a marvelous being. The cunning on this one was so strong that he was able to form a council of lesser gods who would follow and make war against those who created him. The warfare and power of this being were amongst the hierarchy of the leaders of heaven. Rivaled only by a select few spirits and the creator himself. Each spirit uses its particular set of skills to make war with each other, to destroy what was holy from the beginning. They had breastplates of steel along with swords and spears. They were as fast as the speed of light, utilizing lightning as means to attack and thunder as means to destroy. From an earlier epic, the following is recorded for all eyes to see. "To assist her, Ninurta from his Storm bird withering beams at the enemy's strongholds shot, iskur from the skies with scorching lightning and smashing thunders attacked." (See the writings of Zechariah Sitchins) Frost and heat and fire, along with the skill of the world's most renowned fighters, were all placed in opposition against those equally of the same fashion. Although their powers were great, they couldn't prevail against the Spirits of Light. The Gods of Order were able to win the war in spectacular fashion. No matter how hard the dragon and his gods may have fought, there was nothing that could stop what was inevitable.

In my educated hypothesis, the separation between good and evil, light and dark, just and unjust, was made here, in the first world. Balancing each other in a perpetual dance of nature and life. The dragon was cast out of the first world and out of heaven. The ancient legend says the creator made the dragon perfect in all his ways until sin was found in him. There is a funny thing about sin or evil. It is easy to differentiate when there is only one individual drawing the line between them, being the deciding factor. Let me give you an example in the movie Thor. It goes over the realms and how Thor and his counterparts are the protectors of all the realms. The lead realm is Asgard, which is the kingdom. This movie is highly based on Norse mythology and the tales of the great Odin and the paradise of Valhalla. Once again, each of the warriors has a particular set of skills. They are Gods of their own abilities; do you see the correlation? They all fight differently but nonetheless are very dangerous, using different powers to subdue their enemies. These warriors from Asgard would eventually go to the earth and be hailed as gods! Loki, Thor's brother, ultimately tries to rule Earth and corrupt it. This is similar to what happened in the beginning of time before the earth was even created and man was formed. Loki (which is the dragon) would cause a war in heaven and be cast out to the earth. According to the text, he would devise a plan to deceive the earth and gain power. These movies and cartoons show certain things that are similar to what actually happened in the legends and myths of old for a reason. Fairy Tales aren't always fairy tales.

So, the dragon and his gods were cast to the earth. No longer would the dragon be allowed to dwell in the lofty and holy. His dwelling place would be the 2nd world. The mundane reality in comparison to the substantial reality. It would be the world that has yet to be corrupted. A world that has not known any bloodshed, only peace and tranquility. As the scripture states and expresses the severity of what is about to befall this realm, woe unto those who inhabit the earth. "Therefore, rejoice ye heavens and ye that dwell in them. Woe to the inhibitors of the earth and the sea for the devil is come down unto you having great wrath because he knoweth that he has but a short time" (see the book of Revelation). These beings who were cast out were labeled "watchers" by the old hierophants. Our modern-day scholars and archeologists have now identified these beings as aliens. They are also referred to as the Sons of Anuk. These modern masters of ancient knowledge have seen much evidence supporting claims of the earth being visited by these fallen angels, besides only the papyrus of the common era. The modern term extra-terrestrial is very common amongst the scientific community. What most people fail to realize is the synchronicities between the identification of these beings. No matter what the name or the story behind them is, the birth of such a legend is always the same.

Most of the ancient heroes and mighty warriors all throughout the world, between diverse cultures and habitations, wrote about being taken. According to the writings of Zechariah Sitchin, the gods may have done this often to many of the ancient demigods. "As the battles raged on and on, sometimes pitching one hero against another, the gods, too, kept a watchful eye over individual warriors. Swooping down to snatch away a beleaguered or to steer a driverless chariot." We can also synchronize legends of the prophets being taken on whirlwinds, not being able to tell whether their soul is still tethered to the body or separated. These beings would appear to mankind throughout the generations and give the leaders of that civilization knowledge. Some believe this knowledge was given to advance mankind, while others believe the knowledge that is given is only to hinder the creation. In my opinion, this fierce battle was not over because the dragon and his angels had been cast out of heaven. According to most religions and even the Dead Sea Scrolls, the world is awaiting an end of days cataclysm or war. In my studies of the philosophies of different sects, I have found that the scriptures and holy texts can be interpreted in seven ways. The literal is the first and lowest understanding, so I can only conclude the initial battle was just the surface. If we entertain this perspective of the fall of the gods from heaven, we must agree the dragon knew god's creation very well. All because he is a creation himself, highly intellectual, one of the wisest beings ever created, with supernatural advanced technology and power of the secrets of the universe; he knew that it would only take a push in chaos to create that same divide he created in the first world.

The corruption of mankind began, and that same divide, which took place in the first world, also occurred in the second world. This divide is that of war and peace, good and evil. This corruption was a particular event on par with the genetic manipulation of man about 200 thousand years ago in terms of a world-changing dynamic etched in history. This event is recorded in almost all religions as well as in secular history; however, in secular history, the turning point is counted merely as a fairy tale. This is somewhat correct, but as we stated earlier in this writing, all fairytales or legends are true in some ways. I know everyone has heard about the show Ancient Aliens. In this show, the topic of discussion circles around both theoretical ideas based upon fact, proof, and prophecy and personal hypothesis, which, according to the accolades of most of the guests on the show, this information can widely be believed. World-renowned scientists, historians, philosophers, and archeologists alike all agree and believe Aliens visited the earth. These scientists and historians believe aliens or the Annunaki came down to earth about 450 thousand years ago, kick-starting civilization and giving mankind certain secrets. These secrets included how to harness energy, the manipulation of plants and wellness regarding health, the idea of flying machines such as airplanes or helicopters, and much more.

The book of Enoch, which is corroborated by the Bible, teaches us that a group of fallen angels descended on the earth and began polluting humankind. We went over that fall earlier with the Hebraic version of the first war to ever take place in time, but just to reiterate, let me give you the reference. "And it came to pass, when the sons of men had increased, that in those days there were born to them fair and beautiful daughters. And the Angels, the sons of Heaven, saw them and desired them. And they said to one another: "Come, let us choose for ourselves wives, from the children of men, and let us beget for ourselves, children." (See the writings of Enoch) According to the older version of the story written originally on tablets of lapis lazuli, a deep blue metamorphic crystal, and semi-precious stone, A different race of Aliens, different from the Bloodline of Anu, came down and carried out this act. "Unbeknownst to the leaders on earth, a multitude of Igigi on Lahmu got together. What to Marduk is permitted, from us too should not be deprived! To each other, they said, enough suffering and loneliness offspring not ever having, Was their slogan. During their comings and goings between Lahmu and Earth, the daughters of the Earthlings, the Adapite Females as them they called, they saw, and after them, they lusted; and to each other, the plotters said: Come let us choose wives from among the Adapite Females, and children begat." (See the Lost Book of Enki)

So, the beings that were created on the first day of the first world had fallen, and according to legend, they mated with women. This union between God and man caused the manipulation of the Gene pool. Hence, the Demi-gods and all the great tales of the Titans and warriors of Renown. One of the most famous Demigods of old was that of Achilles, son of Peleus, king of Myrmidons, and his legendary victory on the sands of

Troy. According to the Encyclopedia of Britannica, Achilles obtained armor from the god Hephaestus and, after famously slaying Prince Hector where he stood, brutally dragged his corpse behind his chariot. In Homer's writings, the Greek storyteller, we find that this war was instigated by the god Zeus, who corresponds with Jove, Jupiter, or Enlil, the highest god on earth. "There was a time when thousands upon thousands of men encumbered the broad bosom of the earth. And having pity on them, Zeus in his great wisdom resolved to lighten Earth's burden, so he caused the strife at Illion (Troy) to that end; that through death he might make a void in the race of men." Zechariah Sitchin writes, "Homer, the Greek storyteller who related the war's events in the Illiad, blamed the whim of the gods for instigating the conflict and for turning and twisting it to its ultimate major proportions." Besides the fact that the battles of men have been the playing constructs of the gods, we see here that the gods would fight side by side with men to the death. In fact, the Dead Sea Scrolls foretell that exact sentiment. "On that day, the company of the Divine and the congregation of the Mortals shall engage side by side in combat and carnage. The sons of light shall battle against the sons of darkness with a show of god-like might, amid uproarious tumult, amid the war cries of gods and men."

Another example of a great battle between the gods and demigods is Gilgamesh, who was two-thirds divine and one-third human. He was the son of King Lugalbanda and the son of the Goddess Ninsun, and he was a fierce and great warrior. There are many perspectives concerning Gilgamesh to have been the biblical Nimrod. Interestingly the Bible calls Nimrod a Great king and Mighty Hunter before the lord. According to the Tablets of Enki, Gilgamesh was favored by Enlil, Lord of the Edin. I would like to point out the clear synchronism. Gilgamesh was Powerful, violent, and splendid, a wild bull of a man admired by his soldiers. Standing over 9 feet tall, Gilgamesh was said to have muscles of steel, having been unvanquished in battle. One of the most exciting tales of his adventures was the battle between Humbaba, the guardian of the great Cedar Forrest of the gods. This Humbaba was a fierce monster with razor sharp teeth, unmeasurable height, and power; it was employed to terrify men from entering the Cedar Garden by Enlil, the lord of the earth, who is the great Anunnaki deity of old. The Cedar Forrest was the landing place high in the mountains for the gods. Particularly, the region of the Cedar Mountains belonged to Enlil. This Forrest is similar to the Garden of Eden written in Hebraic history. We know that Enlil, or the god of the bible, placed an angel with a flaming sword at the entrance of the famed mythical garden in order to stop the first humans from eating the Tree of Life and living forever. Gilgamesh the Demi-god, along with his companion Enkidu the brave, who was a bloodless cyborg fashioned from the hands of the gods, waged war with the monster of the cedar Forrest, ultimately ending in the demise of the monster!

"Enkidu said, you have never met him, so you do not know the horror that lurks ahead, but when I saw him, my blood ran cold. His teeth are razor sharp, and they stick out like tusks; his face, blood smeared, is a lion face; he charges ahead like a raging torrent, his forehead ablaze. Who can withstand him? I am terrified. I cannot go on. Gilgamesh said, courage, dear brother, this is no time to give into fear. We have come so far across the mountains, and our journey is about to reach its goal. You were raised in the wild, and with your own hands, you have killed marauding lions and wolves; you are brave, and your heart has been tested in combat. Though your arms feel weak now and your legs tremble, you are a warrior; you know what to do. Shout out your battle cry and let your voice sound like a kettle drum. Let your heart inspire you to be joyous in battle, to forget about death. If we help each other and fight side by side, we will make a lasting name for ourselves; we will stamp our fame on men's minds forever. They walked deep into the cedar forest, gripping their axes and their knives unsheathed, following the trail that Humbaba had made. They came within sight of the monster's den. He was waiting inside it. Their blood ran cold. He saw two friends; he grimaced, he bared his teeth, and he let out a deafening roar. He glared at Gilgamesh, young man he said, you will never go home; prepare to die. Dread surged through Gilgamesh; terror flooded his muscles, his heart froze, his mouth went dry, his legs shook, and his feet were rooted to the ground.

Enkidu saw his dismay and said, Dear friend, the great warrior and noble hero, do not lose courage; remember this: two boats lashed together will never sink. A three-ply rope is not easily broken. If we help each other fight side by side, what harm can come to us? Let us go on. They advanced to the monster's den. Humbaba charged out, roaring at them, and said, I know you, Gilgamesh. Do not be a fool. Go away. Leave the Cedar Forrest. Have madmen told you to come here? I will tear you limb from limb. I will crush you and leave you bloody and mangled on the ground. And you, Enkidu, you son of a fish or turtle. You gutless, fatherless spawn who never suckled on mothers' milk, I saw you in the pastures while you were young; I saw you graze with the wandering herds, but I did not kill you; you were too scrawny. You would not have made a decent meal. And now you dare to lead Gilgamesh here; you both stand before me looking like a pair of frightened girls. I will slit your throats; I will cut off your heads; I will feed your stinking guts to the shrieking vultures and crows. Gilgamesh backed away. He said, how dreadful Humbaba's face has become! It is changing into a thousand nightmares faced, more horrible than I can bear. I feel haunted. I am too afraid to go on. Enkidu answered why, dear friend, do you speak like a coward? What you just said is unworthy of you. It grieves my heart. We must not hesitate or retreat. Two intimate friends cannot be defeated. Be courageous. Remember how strong you are. I will stand by you. Now, let us attack. Gilgamesh felt his courage return. They charged at Humbaba like two wild bulls. The monster let out a defining cry, and his roar boomed forth like a blast of thunder. He stamped, and the ground burst open; his steps split the mountains of Lebanon, the clouds turned black, and a sulfurous fog descended on them and made their eyes ache. Then Shamash threw strong winds at Humbaba, the south wind, the north wind, the east, and the west, storm wind, gale wind, hurricane, tornado, to pin him down and paralyze his steps; he could not move forward; he could not retreat. Gilgamesh saw it; he leaped upon him, and he held a knife to Humbaba's throat."

This battle between the Monster of the gods and the Demi-god king was fierce yet swift, ending in brutal fashion. "Knowing he was doomed, Humbaba cried out, and I curse you both because you have done this. May Enkidu die, may he die in great pain, may Gilgamesh be inconsolable, may his merciless heart be crushed with grief. Gilgamesh dropped his axe, appalled. Enkidu said, Courage, dear friend. Close your ears to Humbaba's curses. Do not listen to a word. Slaughter him. Now! Gilgamesh, hearing his beloved friend, came to himself. He yelled; he lifted his massive axe, he swung it, and it tore into Humbaba's neck; the blood shot out, again the axe bit flesh and bone; the monster staggered, his eyes rolled, and at the axe third stroke, he toppled like a cedar and crashed to the ground. At his death, the mountains of Lebanon shook, the valleys ran with his blood for ten miles, and the Forrest resounded. Then the two friends sliced him open, pulled out his intestines, cut off his head with his knife-sharp teeth and horrible bloodshot staring eyes."

The great Demi king Gilgamesh and his companion waged war against the monster of Lord Enlil, forever scribing their name in the minds and hearts of men and gods. Had it not been for Shamas (the god Utu), maybe these heroes would not have succeeded in this great fight. Most, if not all, of these battles between humankind and demigods alike all stem from the un-seen hand of higher beings in the higher realms. As stated in the writings of the epistles, we do not fight against flesh and blood but against principalities and powers of spiritual wickedness in high places. These beings operate on full power vehemently expressed within the lower realms, meaning they can be tangible and intangible, spiritual and physical. According to the tablets, in ancient times, there were sky cities above the high and lofty mountain peaks, and great aquatic cities beneath the depths of the seas. Some of these were abodes, others were fortresses of war carrying out battle! "These wars were fought on land, in the air, and beneath the seas. The Asuras, according to the Mahabharata, made for themselves three metal fortresses in the skies, from which they attacked the three regions of the earth. Their allies in the war of the gods could become invisible and used invisible weapons; and others fought from a city beneath the sea, which they had captured from the gods." These mountain peaks were but landing points and resting places for the celestial boats, sky birds, and whirlwinds of the ancient gods. A counsel of the order by rank was set up between these beings, where deliberation of agenda was in full effect. These powers are over the political systems, government structures, monarchs, and priesthoods, and the influence of their decisions affected the entire habitation of the earthlings. This is why when we read the ancient writings of the Hebrews within the apocalypse and testament of Abraham, the god of the underworld in the form of a black bird speaks to Abraham, asking him why he is treading upon the domain of the gods which are the high and lofty mountain tops, mere mortals cannot tread upon holy land without divine interference. "And an unclean bird flew down on the carcasses and I drove it away, and the unclean bird spoke to me and said, what are you doing, Abraham on the holy heights where no one eats or drinks, nor is there food upon them for men." (See the apocalypse of Abraham)

Securely written in the memoirs of Lord Enki, we find that each political system or kingdom legislature has an allotted time to rule corresponding to cosmic star alignment. Thus, it will fall and rise accordingly. "Did not the era of Marduk in the heavens arrive?" Marduk was known as the god Amun Ra in the ancient world, the first-born son of Lord Enki, who was one of the first beings that came to the earth. "Your celestial time in the heavens will come, a station mine adjourning yours shall be." If we look at our King James Bible, we can also see this unforeseen aspect of divinity in play during the prophecies of Daniel. Was the prophet seeing future events of governments, or was there something hidden in the dream vision? Let us look more into some legends concerning the battles of these great beings to see if we can find a clue. As we dive deeper and deeper into the ancient tablets, we run into the writings of one of the most influential authors of the Piscean age, allegedly recorded by man from a god for a time such as this. Often, throughout the natural course of events, the past becomes mirrored in the future. Many incidents seem to repeat themselves, such as the rise and fall of nations and kingdoms. This is a question the gods ask themselves after contemplating the course of events that led to destruction in ancient times. Was it fate or destiny? They inquired of each other, Enlil, and Enki.

Corresponding with the stars, written Inside the codex DNA of humans are past failures, past achievements, past traumas, and past contentment, which teach us valuable lessons for the future or even the present now. The battles of the gods of the past give us a glimpse into prehistoric sacred arts and sciences, mingled with alien martial art techniques that brought about much calamity amongst the earthlings and the gods who created us. Battles that would lead to the massacre of ancient Sumer, which was so catastrophic and devastating that it wiped out the entire population. This could correlate to an event in the bible between Sodom and Gomorrah and its extinction being of

Radiological proportions. In Delores Cannon's writings, we find very intriguing evidence of nuclear activity. Geologists' investigations conclude that there are traces of petroleum and uranium in the same area where it is said that this event took place. Interesting. According to Zechariah Sitchin and his writings, the Anunnaki had martial arts contests between its heroes. It is here where a man can begin to imagine the difference in technical disciplines between each hero martial artist. Maybe this competition was in an Olympic fashion or professional setting like what we have today, whether it be for financial gain and glory or for spirit and technique. The martial arts competitions between the gods not only answer the question of having recorded evidence of the art on other worlds, but the cosmic origin once again proves prevalent. In the ancient language of Akkadian, the goddess Ishtar is associated with the planet Venus but originally known as Innana, a descendant of Lord Enlil, is a warrior princess highly skilled and favored amongst her peers and in martial arts. Known as the goddess of love, she is not short of raging warfare on other gods and earthlings in the olden times, spilling much bloodshed of various cults and sects after the death of her beloved espoused husband. "Innana by her parents Nannar and Ningal was beloved, Enlil by her cradle sat. Beautiful beyond describing she was, in martial arts with Anunnaki heroes, she competed. Of journeys in the heavens and of celestial boats from her brother Utu she learned; A sky ship of her own, to roam in earth skies to her the Anunnaki presented." (See the Lost Book of Enki)

Later, in the memoirs of Lord Enki, the warrior princess Ishtar battles Amun Ra for supremacy in an epic sky war.

Celestial warships equipped with weapons of energy manipulation and missiles were being used in this great battle. Her exploits can be examined more intently should we decide to go further into the story, but for now, this will conclude her tale. Correspondingly, it is also recorded that Horus an Egyptian deity was also versed in Martial arts. "Horus grew up as a Netch-atef, "Avenger of his Father." Educated and trained in martial arts by goddesses and gods who sided with Osiris, he was groomed as a divine prince worthy of association." (See The wars of gods and men) Wrestling and hand-to-hand combat were not only used by the gods who came to Earth but also in the home-world of the fallen angels themselves! If we search the ancient legends, we can find tales of the royal Anunnaki King and God of all gods, Anu, using both wrestling and hand-to-hand combat to obtain his throne and later defend it! "In the ninth shar, Anu gave battle to Alalu. To hand-to-hand combat with bodies naked, Alalu he challenged. Let the winner be king, Anu said. They grappled with each other in the public square; doorposts trembled, and walls shook." Even the king and leader of the Alien Race used a form of martial arts for the contest of succession. The battles of the gods end written in time, inscribed on clay, and illustriously illustrated through hieroglyphs and symbology, but most importantly, the information is embedded and stored in the cosmos for all to see.

The modern age has recorded its own battles, and we will never know if the gods still have an unseen hand in the affairs of humanity. Until such a time when the gods reveal themselves, curiosity will be the catalyst that removes ignorance and lifts the veil. If there is one thing that is certain, it is this. There is no question that Martial Arts is not from this planet. It is the art that truly began in the heavens. What was looked upon as merely one of the most ancient ways of expression has now become more of a cosmic universal mystery. There is no denial of its cosmic nature. Religion wrote about it, spirituality lives it, and you must become it. The history of the world we strive to know, but even history has a way of changing throughout time. My goal as a philosopher and martial artist is to find a way to exist as myself but ever-changing into another. As we enter the age of the water bearer, the intellectual gods will favor us. Man can choose himself to wonder about aimlessly, or should he wake up from his slumber? If the latter is the case, then let this treatise be a record of light and rebellion. These are the words of my soul.

Initiate | | *YaRaah SOG*

The art of life and love. The wisdom of ancient souls. The mysteries of illumined informed.

M. J. Walker

PEACE IN DARKNESS

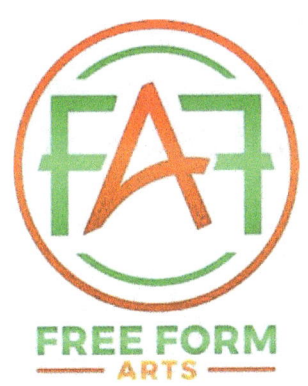

LIFE IN LIGHT